CONTENTS

CW01072390

INTRODUCTION

Buckinghamshire is only a slender strip of England, no more than 27 miles east to west across at its broadest, running from the river Thames near Dorney northwards for just over 50 miles to its border with Northamptonshire a mile and a half north-west of Lavendon. Yet generations have been captivated by the beauty of the ridges and bottoms of the Chilterns, and the fertile river valleys of the Thames, the Colne, the Thame and the Great Ouse that vaguely sketch out the county's boundaries. The beech woods for which the south-east of the county is renowned not only yielded the raw material for wood turners and furniture makers around Chesham and High Wycombe, but are still a glory to be enjoyed by walkers.

The county's beauty and tranquillity has inspired its share of poets too, most famously Thomas Gray, who lived for a time at Stoke Poges where he was moved to compose his *Elegy in a Country Churchyard*. William Cowper, between outpourings of verse and hymns described his chosen village, Weston Underwood, as 'one of the prettiest in the kingdom'. The great John Milton was certainly immune to the county's visual charms, for he was blind when he composed *Paradise Lost* at Chalfont St Giles; but he found something there, if only freedom from the persecution that loomed over him as a Parliamentary loyalist in Restoration England.

Milton, of course, was a political thinker as well as a poet, which was why he had to seek rural asylum. The county has always had strong political connections, in the best sense of the word. No less an authority than Benjamin Disraeli, the great 19th-century prime minister, once declared 'there is something in the air of Bucks favourable to political knowledge and vigour'. He was born in the county himself (and is buried there, too, at Hughenden), the third of Buckinghamshire's three prime ministers – the others were the 18th-century Grenvilles, father and son, the elder of whom did much to provoke the American War of Independence. Disraeli probably had in mind other men, whose ideas revolutionized the governance of the nation. He would certainly have included in those affected by the county's air John Hampden, whose refusal to pay Ship Money to King Charles I gave Parliamentarians a cause to rally in opposition to the Crown and led ultimately to the great tumult of the Civil War. And he might well have considered John Wilkes, one of the founders of modern British radicalism, who lived in Prebendal House, Aylesbury.

EARLY DAYS

It was politics, not topography, that determined the present boundaries of Buckinghamshire – though politics that were debated not in the House of Commons but with sword and byrnie in the

PHILIP'S

COUNTY GUIDE

BUCKINGHAMSHIRE

County Editor Ian Buchanan

Writers:
Adrian Berkeley, Fergus Fleming, David Graham
John Rafferty, Tim Robinson

■

Photography by John Bethell

First published in Great Britain in 1994
by Philip's, an imprint of
Reed Consumer Books Ltd
Michelin House, 81 Fulham Road,
London SW3 6RB
and Auckland, Melbourne, Singapore and
Toronto

Text and maps © Reed International Books Ltd
Pictures © John Bethell
Series Editor: Alan Lothian

Mapping based upon Ordnance Survey maps
with the permission of the Controller of Her
Majesty's Stationery Office
© Crown copyright

ISBN 0 540 05793 2

A CIP catalogue record for this book is available
at the British Library

Printed in Hong Kong

The publishers would like to thank the following
for their advice and assistance during the
preparation of this book:

Bletchley Park Trust
Buckinghamshire County Council (Julian Hunt
    and Jane Cutler)
Buckinghamshire County Museum (Kate
    Hawkins)
Chiltern District Council
Chiltern Open Air Museum Ltd
The Chiltern Society
Cowper and Newton Museum, Olney
Flamingo Gardens and Zoological Park, Weston
    Underwood
Percy Hackling
London Transport Museum (Mark Dennison)
Milton Keynes Borough Council
Milton's Cottage Trust, Chalfont St Giles
Quainton Railway Society
Royal Holloway and Bedford New College
    (Dr Christopher Green)

FURTHER READING

J.R.L. Anderson *The Upper Thames* (Methuen
    1974)
John Camp *Portrait of Buckinghamshire* (Robert
    Hale 1972)
John Julius Norwich *The Architecture of Southern
    England* (Macmillan 1985)
Nikolaus Pevsner *The Buildings of England –
    Buckinghamshire* (Penguin 1960)
Robin Seddon and Rosemary Joekes *The National
    Trust Guide* (Jonathan Cape 1973)
Bruce Watkin *Buckinghamshire: a Shell Guide*
    (Faber 1981)

OTHER TITLES IN THIS SERIES
HAMPSHIRE
OXFORDSHIRE
SURREY
EAST SUSSEX
WEST SUSSEX
see page 160 for details

robust, Anglo-Saxon manner. The story begins in the 9th century, when Alfred the Great of Wessex began the great reorganization of his kingdom needed to fight back against the Danes who held most of north-eastern England as the Danelaw. A treaty defined a political frontier that ran to the old Roman road of Watling Street (roughly, the line of the modern A5) and left the little settlement of Buckingham in a no-man's-land. Perhaps in the hope of using it as a springboard for further advances, the king designated it a county town. Buckingham still needed a county; that was left to Alfred's son, Edward. In preparation for his reconquest of the Danelaw, he ordered two forts to be built at Buckingham in 914 AD. The territory that he assigned for their maintenance amounted in essence if not in name to the Buckinghamshire we know today.

As Alfred's heirs continued the reconquest, they backed it up with administrative reconstruction. It was his grandson Edgar who formally created the shires, which were subdivided into 'Hundreds'. These hundreds were based in turn on a more fundamental unit of land: the 'hide', which was reckoned as the acreage sufficient to sustain a free peasant – a *ceorl* – and his family. The *ceorl* held his land with obligations, notably military duty, and a Hundred, at any rate in theory, was a district of a hundred hides – a useful force. Changes in the boundaries of the hundreds, through inheritance and marriage, made their own contribution to the county's present tortuous outline.

Today, Members of Parliament wishing to resign their seats between General Elections apply for the stewardship of the 'Chiltern Hundreds'. It is a meaningless sinecure today, one of the many cobwebbed oddities on the fringes of the British constitution. The Chiltern Hundreds themselves now include some of the most comfortable commuter villages in Britain. Once, though, that stewardship was one of the toughest jobs in the kingdom: the Chiltern Hundreds, set amid the forest tracks of southern Buckinghamshire, were outlaw country par excellence.

GEOGRAPHY

Geographically, the shape of the county makes little logical sense: it cuts across at least four distinct regions. In accord with the rest of southern England, the geological structure of the county runs broadly north-east to south-west, with its major feature, the Chiltern Hills, bisecting the southern half of the county. Going south from its most northern point, the traveller crosses the flat Ouse valley on which Olney, Newport Pagnell, Stony Stratford and the old county capital of Buckingham stand, before entering the undulating landscape typified by the hunting territory of Whaddon Chase south-west of Milton Keynes. From there, the Vale of Aylesbury stretches south again to the Chilterns, whose approaching escarpment can be seen for miles, as it rises dramatically from the edge of the Vale. From the escarpment's high points at Coombe Hill, Aston Hill and Ivinghoe Beacon, a southbound traveller's backward glance is rewarded by a wonderful panorama. From these heights, the hills descend gently for 20 miles, with chalk ridges and bottoms giving way to the gravel of river terraces and the Thames itself, the county's southern boundary.

GEOLOGICAL FOUNDATIONS
On a geological timescale, Buckinghamshire is young: it spent most of the last 200 million years lying quietly beneath shallow seas. Between 170 and 140 million years ago, in the period known by geologists as the Jurassic, great rivers chewed at the older rocks of northern Europe and carried them as silt far out above what would one day be England. There, the silt settled, forming the Kimmeridge, Oxford and London clay beds that lie from south of the Great Ouse to the Thames valley.

The seas deposited more than silt: much of the life with which they teemed fixed in shells and skeletons the calcium carbonate that time compressed into the oolitic limestone on which Aylesbury stands and which raises Oving, Wing and Whitchurch above the level of the plain. Here and there, these ancient creatures have been preserved in something of their original form, as in the walls surrounding Hartwell House, where giant ammonite fossils serve as ornamental brickwork.

The end of the Jurassic period was marked by a greatly reduced silt flow, which ended clay formation but led to clear waters open to sunlight. The light encouraged the growth of marine creatures; their remains, unmixed with the assorted minerals of the silt, became the thick layer of chalk that now forms the Chilterns and caps Brill Hill. At a rate of around an inch every 2,500 years, the slow creation of those chalk upland ridges, which were to become the highways of the first inhabitants and played such a vital role in the human development of the region, required something like 25 million years. Those clear Cretaceous seas were also home to sponge-like creatures, which the process of fossilization turned into nodules of flint; one of man's first commodities.

ICE AGES
At the end of the Cretaceous (from the Latin word for chalk) Era, around 65 million years ago, those parts of Great Britain that stood above the waters were still joined to Europe, itself attached to North America; the Thames was a tributary of the Rhine, which emptied into the North Sea near what is now the Dogger Bank. By some 30 million years ago the region had been largely formed; continental collisions had raised the Alps, tilted southern England and buckled the land to lift the Chilterns, a process that is still continuing today.

There was also a dramatic change in climate. Over a long period, the polar ice-cap advanced and retreated many times, and much of northern Europe was subjected the grinding process of glaciation. Sea levels fell as the ice-cap thickened; the land that would be southern England emerged from the waters. In inter-glacial periods, when the ice partly receded for a spell, the landscape would have been much like the tundra of modern Arctic Siberia, locked in permafrost.

During its southernmost incursions, the ice-cap covered much of north Buckinghamshire. Its detritus remains, in the form of the drift deposits of boulder clay and glacial gravel that give the area around Whaddon Chase its rolling profile.

FIRST INHABITANTS

Around a quarter of a million years ago, the first human inhabitants appeared in Buckinghamshire: stone axes from the Acheulian culture (of around 300,000 years ago) have been found in the valley of the Thame, on river terraces above the Thames between Taplow and Slough, and in the Chilterns at gravel diggings near Burnham. Other Stone Age artefacts have been unearthed on the banks of the Wye in High Wycombe, and at Princes Risborough. Settlement was probably cyclic, over the millennia. During inter-glacial periods, these prehistoric hunters would have followed their prey here as the ice and snow loosened their grip and allowed game to migrate north. When the ice creaked south once more, their descendants would be driven back. But the journey from the mainland, at least, presented no difficulties: Southern England remained connected to continental Europe until around 8,000 years ago.

The last glacial period began to end around 20,000 years ago, leaving the land in more or less its present form, and by around 12,000 BC the climate was warm enough for all of southern Britain to attract human colonization. Mesolithic (Middle Stone Age) settlers are thought to have come from Europe by way of the Rhine and the Thames; they were skilled in the use of boats and exploited the rivers as their main highways.

In Buckinghamshire's high chalk ridges, they found other natural pathways: their shallow, quick-draining soil made for scrubby heathland that gave both easy passage and good visibility against marauders, animal or fellow-human. The Upper Icknield Way across the Chilterns was well-known to the Neolithic (New Stone Age) settlers, who brought improved pottery and advanced agricultural skills. By the time they arrived, from the Mediterranean around 3500 BC, Britain was an island; whether they sailed in from the west, by the Bristol Channel, or from the south and east, across the English Channel, is still unknown.

Once inland, though, they certainly used routes that ran through the valleys carved through the Chilterns by the Wye, the Misbourne and the Chess. One such path led from Saunderton on the Icknield Way via High Wycombe to Bourne End on the Thames, as evidenced by Neolithic tools that have been found at High Wycombe, Iver, Bledlow and Whiteleaf. At Whiteleaf Hill, above Icknield Way, is a kidney-shaped burial chamber dating from the Neolithic age, which has provided archaeological evidence of an overlap in occupation by Middle and New Stone Age cultures.

Whoever introduced metallurgy to Buckinghamshire, the metals themselves certainly came from elsewhere, for the county has never had ore deposits of its own. Bronze first arrived as finished goods from manufacturing centres in Ireland, Scotland, Northern England and North Wales but as bronze-smiths increased in number, a trade in metal ingots for making goods locally developed. Copper came mostly from Anglesey and Ireland, which was also the source of gold, and tin came from Cornwall. With this growing demand, the trade routes across the Chilterns were used more and more.

IRON AGE

British smiths began using iron from around 650 BC; again, the appearance of iron artefacts, once thought the sign of an influx or invasion by a 'superior' race, is more likely to have been simply the learning by the indigenous people of a new technology. Ores from which iron might be smelted were more easily available than those of copper or tin, although the techniques involved, requiring much higher temperatures, were a good deal more difficult.

From around 600 BC, possibly connected with the growth in trade, there was a great increase in the number of defended sites. The long-distance footpath, the Ridgeway, itself following an ancient line, links together a number of important hillforts as it passes through the county on its way to Avebury in Wiltshire. The best-preserved of these can still be seen on Beacon Hill at Ivinghoe, where the footpath begins, and at Pulpit Hill, above Great Kimble.

From the 5th century down to near the end of the 3rd century BC, the people of the future Buckinghamshire had close ties with Europe, with goods and ideas travelling in both directions. Trade accelerated at the beginning of the 1st century BC, perhaps because of an invasion by a people the Romans knew as the Belgae, who were thought to have introduced coinage and an improved plough that could exploit the heavier soils of lower ground. Once more, present interpretation of the archaeological record seems to indicate a gentler continuum of change, with development coming through gradual assimilation rather than large-scale conquest.

The Belgae sited their defended settlements, or oppida, as the Romans called them, on lower ground in preference to their predecessors' hillforts. They certainly used wheeled chariots and it seems certain that good quality tracks existed to ride them on. It is possible that the Lower Icknield Way came into use at the time wheeled transport was introduced. Evidence of Belgic occupation has been found at Bulstrode Park, Gerrards Cross, which is the largest Iron Age fort in the county, and at Medmenham.

According to Julius Caesar, writing about his conquest of Gaul, one of the Belgic tribes, the Catuvellauni, ruled the part of England that includes Buckinghamshire. One of the Catuvellauni's most famous kings, Cunobelinus, whom we remember as Cymbeline, died around 40 AD, leaving his two sons to rule. Caratacus reigned south of the Thames and Togodumnus north. It fell to them to oppose the Claudian invasion of the region, which began in 43 AD. They were defeated by the Roman commander, Aulus Plautius; Togodumnus was killed and Caratacus was sent as a captive to Rome.

ROMAN AND SAXON

The Roman subjugation of Britain was a long-drawn affair, with hillforts sometimes having to be overcome one at a time. The Romans gradually consolidated their gains, built fortified camps of their own and, above all else, roads. The longevity of these roads would have astonished the Roman engineers. Almost 2,000 years later, the route followed by many modern highways is an impressive testimony to their skills. Chief among them is Watling Street, now the A5, and Akeman Street, now the A41.

The Romans ended the old British tribal kingdoms, but they brought the advantages of peace and stable government in their stead. Buckinghamshire was probably a net gainer: certainly, the abundance of remains from the period of the Roman occupation demonstrates that the area was quite densely populated.

Roman power collapsed in the 4th century AD, when the legions were recalled to defend Rome itself. Germanic tribes, loosely known as the Saxons, had begun raiding during the last century of Roman occupation, and now their depredations increased. By the 5th century, they were ready to turn from brief forays bent on loot to conquest and permanent settlement.

The Anglo-Saxon Chronicle records the capture of Aylesbury from the Britons, following the battle of 'Bedconford' (Bedford) in 571, at around which time most of Buckinghamshire would have become part of the kingdom of Mercia. The Anglo-Saxon invasion, as with previous invasions, was a lengthy business, with assimilation probably more important than massacre as the new rulers imposed themselves and their culture upon their weaker prey. The heavily-wooded nature of much of Buckinghamshire probably made the process there even slower than elsewhere: historians have postulated the survival of a substantial British enclave in the Chilterns until the end of the 7th century.

The Saxons built in wood and at first cremated their dead, later burying them in graves unmarked by mounds or monuments. Thus little is left for us to remember them by. Even Grim's Ditch, near Great Hampden, which has long been considered to be a Saxon relic, is now thought by some archaeologists to date from the Iron Age. Among the few visible signs of the Anglo-Saxon centuries *are* some surviving field systems, such as those to be seen at Cheddington. And after the return of Christianity, which had first come in Roman times and lingered on in its Celtic form, some Saxon Churches were built solidly enough to stand until the present day. All Saints' Church in Wing, erected early in the 10th century, is the best remaining example.

Scarcity of building material was one reason for the dearth of solid construction. The geological resources of the county included little in the way of easily extractable stone or minerals. The shortage of stone helps explain the absence of great cathedrals or castles; but on the other hand, the great abundance and variety of clays generated a brick-making industry that has traditionally provided the raw materials that built the county.

Good Buckinghamshire clay is also the main constituent of witchert, a local building material made from a hard, chalky earth found a foot or two below the surface in a mile-wide belt stretching westwards from near Aylesbury to Long Crendon. Mixed with water and straw, this chalky earth becomes a material solid enough to build walls two to three feet wide on a rubblestone plinth, a technique that results in the rounded walls seen, for example, at Lower Winchendon.

THE NORMANS AND AFTER
After some centuries of relative tranquillity during which Christianity was re-established throughout the Saxon kingdoms and their churches and religious centres enriched with treasures of gold and silver, a new threat emerged. Scandinavian raiders launched ferociously violent attacks on the remote and unprotected, as well as richly endowed, monastic colonies around the coast of Britain and Ireland. Like the Saxons before them, some of the raiders decided to stay. By 865 the Danes began a wholesale invasion of Northumbria and eastern England; only Wessex under King Alfred managed to hold out against the onslaught, and as we have seen, Buckingham was a frontier post. But although the king's successors set up the shires as we know them, the Saxon line had not long to run. The Norman invasion and the decisive battle of Hastings in 1066 brought an abrupt end to Anglo-Saxon Buckinghamshire.

After William's victory, his commanders were rewarded by gifts of land. At Beachampton, a few remains of a manor house given in such a way are still to be seen, while Norman churches are to be found all over the county. Less ancient churches have often preserved Norman accoutrements, like the baptismal fonts at St James's, Bierton; Holy Trinity, Bledlow; St Nicholas's, Great Kimble; St Mary's, Hambleden; and St Nicholas's, Ibstone. There is a beautifully preserved Norman doorway at Chantry Chapel in Buckingham. At Weston Turville and at Wing there are still some remnants of motte and bailey castles, mostly built of earth and wood, although Bolebec Castle, at Whitchurch, was, unusually for Buckinghamshire, built of stone.

In the years after the Conquest, the former Saxon stronghold of Buckingham declined in importance; in Tudor times, Henry VIII decreed that its status as county town should pass to the more centrally placed Aylesbury.

MATERIALS AND INDUSTRY
Buckinghamshire, as has been seen, is deficient in good building stone, with limited limestone quarrying to the west of Aylesbury and

the somewhat ostentatiously named 'Buckingham marble', in reality an inferior form of limestone, found in small quantities further north. Flint, one of the few suitable materials available in any abundance, has been used widely for building, but most stone has always been expensively transported from elsewhere. The dearth of good building stone has been a great encouragement to brick-making, which has made its mark all over the county in one way or another.

Brill Common bears the scars of clay-working over hundreds of years and at Great Linford, restored brick-making kilns can be seen. At Newton Longville the tall chimneys of The London Brick Company, which ceased production only in 1990, are visible for miles around. A large variety of poetically-named bricks, which included Yellow Cutters, Grissels, Shuffs, Burnovers, Batts, Pale Seconds and Paviours were produced over many years and used to great visual effect throughout Buckinghamshire.

Other than brick-making, industry in the county has always tended to be small-scale, often employing families working together from home. Lace-making, believed to have been brought to the county by Catherine of Aragon in the early 16th century, was a particularly successful example. Buckinghamshire lacemakers became very skilful and their work was considered the finest available. Machine-made Nottingham lace led to the industry's decline from around 1835, though it continued in a small way until after the First World War.

Early in the 18th century, straw-plaiting was introduced to supply the hat-makers of Luton, and grew to become an important part of the local economy around Wing. Straw-plaiting had died out completely by the 1930s and all that now remains of the industry is an ingenious straw-splitting tool invented by a schoolboy in 1813, which is to be seen in some of the county's museums. Wood-turning and furniture-making were established in the beech woods around Chesham and High Wycombe from around 600 years ago. Today, High Wycombe is still a centre for furniture-making, though it too has become less important over recent years.

TRANSPORT

Although it lies close to London, Buckinghamshire was for most of its history insulated to a degree by the great Middlesex forests. From the Middle Ages, the building and upkeep of roads and bridges was organized by Lords of the Manor, sometimes financed by charitable individuals. From 1555 the parishes assumed responsibility, but the charge levied for the roads was regarded as an imposition and their condition deteriorated. In the 18th century, Turnpike Trusts were established between Aylesbury and surrounding towns and road improvements were paid for out of tolls charged on people and goods using them. Aylesbury was on the main coaching route, Akeman Street, which connected London to Oxford, Birmingham and Cambridge. Stony Stratford became an important staging post on Watling Street, running as it has since Roman times from London to

Chester. The arrival of the railways from 1840 led to a gradual decline in coaching as an important means of transport, but coaching inns are still to be found in Amersham, Buckingham, Chalfont St Giles and Chesham.

The building of the Grand Union Canal, by allowing the transport of heavy goods, greatly helped the development of trade. John Westcar of Whitchurch, who died in 1833, is still remembered as the first man to send cattle to Smithfield Market by canal. A branch connecting Aylesbury to the Grand Union at Marsworth opened in 1814. Improved transport has finally resolved the paradoxical nature of Buckinghamshire. The ancient roadways that have done so much to determine its character did not lead to the county: they passed through it. Those who settled there found a place that was safely isolated by the barrier of the Chilterns; yet the highways that crossed them brought a steady stream of travellers and traders, who made it relatively easy to stay in touch with a wider world.

The barrier began to come down at the hands of the 19th-century engineers, pushing their canals and railways steadily onwards. But once again the motive was to move goods from the great manufacturing centres and ports through the county to markets in the cities. Those new highways had a profound effect, of course, bringing new commercial opportunities to the county. The coming of the railways brought speedier access, particularly to London. The Metropolitan Line was quick to exploit the potential of its links to Amersham, Chesham and Chalfont and Latimer for new settlement. The company combined property development with railway management to create what its publicity proudly described as 'Metroland': leafy suburbs in the sanctuary of the Chilterns. It was a new kind of Buckinghamshire.

In the 1960s, a newer version still was created in the form of the new town of Milton Keynes, in some ways a social equivalent of the fast, convenient motorways that were beginning to spread through the land. The town, new grafted on to old and largely populated with urban overspill from London and elsewhere, has been a triumphant success. The M1, the M25 and the M40 have replaced the railways as the great bringers of change; the railways in turn replaced the turnpikes, and before the turnpikes, there were the ancient ways. More people travel through the county than ever before. But not all hurtle onwards: many have come to stay. The quiet valleys that first attracted stone-age hunters may be more accessible now, but they are still there.

Ian Buchanan,
Hook Norton, 1993

LISTINGS & SYMBOLS

LISTINGS

The A–Z of Towns & Villages lists all significant settlements as well as some other places (e.g. Coombe Hill). Smaller hamlets may appear in **bold type** under the heading of a near neighbour. In such cases, the minor locality will also be found in the index.

Cross references to entries in the A–Z are given in SMALL CAPITALS. Cross references to the Days Out section are given in the form 'see p. ...'. **Bold type** is used to highlight important buildings or other features, but does not imply that they are open, or even accessible, to the public.

Details of access and telephone numbers have been provided wherever possible. While every effort has been made to ensure these are up to date, they are subject to change. If you are planning a special trip to visit one of the places listed, it is best to check with the local tourist office in advance.

STAR RATINGS

All entries, and sub-entries within the A–Z, have been rated from 0–3 stars as follows:

★★★	major attraction
★★	general interest
★	local or specialist interest

SYMBOLS

Days Out

⊞	Admission fee
☕	Refreshments
SC	Shop
⚲	Guided tours
♿	Disabled access
♨	Mother and baby facilities
✖	No dogs
🛈	Information centre

A–Z of Towns & Villages

⛪	Church
🏰	Castle
🏛	Historic building
🏛	Museum
M	Monument
☀	Viewpoint
♠	Park or open space
≋	Pond, river or lake
⚱	Pub or inn
🛈	Information centre

ASCOTT HOUSE ★ ★
Map p.150, C3
1 mile E of Wing off the A418

⊞ ⬤ SC ⫽ ⬟ *(gd floor only)* ✕

Built on the site of Ascott Hall, the 17th-century home of the Dormer family, Ascott House is an architectural mixed bag. The old Dormer house, bearing the date 1606 over the door, forms the central part. In 1874 it was bought by Leopold de Rothschild as a hunting box and headquarters for his prized pack of staghounds. The house was extended for Leopold after his purchase, and enlarged again in 1938. Inside are paintings by many English and Dutch masters as well as a number of Rothschild family portraits and collections of Ming porcelain and Chippendale furniture.

Outside, the gardens are one of the last surviving examples of the work of Sir Harry Veitch of Chelsea. Among the attractions are a rock garden, a huge topiary sundial, and an elaborate fountain of Venus by the American sculptor Waldo Story, whose work can also be seen at Cliveden (see p.16) on the Thames. Although the Rothschild family still occupies the house, it was presented to the National Trust in 1950 and is open to the public at the beginning and end of the summer on variable dates. The gardens are also open on selected days between May and August.
National Trust: *0494 528051.*

CHENIES MANOR HOUSE AND GARDEN ★ ★
Map p.147, E3
3 miles E of Amersham off the A404

⊞ ⬤ SC ⫽ ✕

Visitors approach Chenies Manor House by a tree-lined avenue leading from the western side of Chenies village green. Built in the 15th and 16th centuries, it was originally owned by the Cheneys – who also gave their name to the village. But, with the marriage to John Russell in 1526 of the Cheney heiress, the house and its estates came into the possession of the Russells, later the Earls and Dukes of Bedford. The property stayed in Russell hands until 1954, when it was sold to pay the 12th Duke's death duties, and is still in private ownership.

Although its construction pre-dates the Elizabethan era, the red-brick house is very much Elizabethan in appearance. Indeed, both Elizabeth and her father, King Henry VIII, were guests here. A notable feature is the intricate, spiralled brick-work of the many chimneys, which can best be seen from the churchyard at the rear of the house. The number and size of chimney breasts on that particular elevation precluded the use of windows, which gives it an air of dark mystery – a theme that is continued in the interior, where a number of hiding places and secret passages testify to the religious and political turbulence of the time. More peacefully, the house now contains contemporary furnishings and tapestries and a collection of antique dolls.

The beautifully laid-out and cared-for grounds include a white garden, herbaceous borders, a Tudor sunken garden, a 'physic' herb garden with plants both for medical and culinary uses, a Victorian-style kitchen garden, with out-of-the-ordinary vegetables and fruit, two mazes, and a fountain.
Apr–Oct, Wed–Thur 2–5pm; BH Mons 2–6pm; Easter 2–5pm Tel: 0494 762888.

CLAYDON ★ ★ ★
Map p.149, B1
3 miles SW of Winslow off the A413 on minor roads

⊞ ⬤ ⫽ *(parties)* ⬗ ✕

Claydon House has been the home of the Verneys since 1620. Although they gifted the house to the National Trust in 1956, the

The Mercury Fountain, Ascott House

family continues to live in part of it. The house is only a section of a much grander building planned by the second earl in the 18th century, when he tried to make Claydon the most important estate in the county. He spent 40 years and his fortune in an effort to rival Stowe (see p.21), but the project ruined him and he died bankrupt in 1791. Most of the contents were sold off and a great deal of the new work was demolished before completion.

What remains – essentially the south wing of the earl's great project – is still awesome, although the most impressive view is from the main road behind the house rather than its formal entrance. Inside, Claydon has probably the most lavish rococo decoration in the country. The most extraordinary workmanship is in the Chinese room (picture, p.60), where carvings of lace-like intricacy make visitors wonder how such forms were ever conjured from wood.

The house has a strong connection with Florence Nightingale, sister-in-law of Sir Harry Verney. She often stayed at Claydon; her bedroom, along with many letters and mementoes, are on public view.

A large part of the gardens, including the family Church of All Saints, is also open to visitors, and there is a National Trust shop specializing in organic produce. *Apr–Oct daily 1–4.30pm except Tues and Thurs. Tel: 0296 730349.*

CLIVEDEN ★ ★ ★
Map p.142, C1
2 miles N of Taplow off the A4094

£ ♦ *(Wed–Sun)* SC *(Wed–Sun)* ♿ ♨

A sculptured mass of pale stone set upon a vast, brick platform, Cliveden looks down from its lofty eminence above the wooded banks of the Thames towards Cookham, a view that accounts for the proliferation of balconies that garland the house.

It is the third house to stand on the site since 1677; the earliest, scene of the first performance of 'Rule Britannia', was destroyed by fire in 1795; the second was only 20 years old when it suffered the same

fate in 1849. The present house, designed by Sir Charles Barry in 1850, was purchased in 1893 by the controversial, multi-millionaire Astor family, and has since played a greater part in British history than most 19th-century stately homes.

It was the home of Lady Nancy Astor, in 1919 elected as Britain's first woman MP, and in the 1930s, the house became the meeting place of the notorious 'Cliveden Set', a loose grouping of politicians and celebrities who advocated a pro-German policy. Now usually reviled for courting Hitler, the group is still defended by those who claim their efforts were simply an attempt to avert war.

The estate was given to the National Trust in 1942, although members of the Astor family still lived there until 1966. Controversy continued to surround them: in 1963 the house was at the centre of the Profumo scandal, as the scene of lurid goings-on that involved among others the Minister of War, several nightclub 'hostesses' and a Russian diplomat.

Cliveden is now a privately-managed luxury hotel, although the property is still owned by the National Trust. Most of the sumptuous interiors are reserved for residents, but visitors can take tea in some of its former reception rooms. Three rooms – the oak-panelled Grand Hall; the French dining room (with green and gold French panelling that was once part of a chateau owned by Madame Pompadour); and the former library, now a dining room – are open to visitors at all times.

So are the grounds, which are among the finest features of the great house. Formal gardens are set in the midst of subtly-shaped parkland, with broad lawns, hedges in geometric patterns, temples, an amphitheatre and an oriental water garden. Both house and garden are embraced by woodland. Above all, perhaps, there is the incomparable view, the main reason why the house was built in its commanding position.
Grounds: *Daily, Mar–Oct, 11am–6pm; Nov–Dec, 11am–4pm.*
House: *Thurs and Sun, Apr–Oct, 3pm–6pm. Tel: 0628 605069.*

The Memorial Chapel, Cliveden

DORNEY COURT ★★
Map p.142, D2
3 miles NW of Eton on the B3026

Dorney Court is a Tudor manor house of pink-flushed brick, gabled and topped with a pair of tall, ornate chimneys. It seems almost absurdly well preserved, testimony to the considerable amount of restoration work and rebuilding that has continued over many years, and which indeed has offended some purists. However, no visitor should forget that this is a real home, not a museum. Generations of the Palmer family have lived here and cared for it since the early 17th century, and they are the real explanation for Dorney Court's relatively unaged appearance (picture, p.68).

One of the house's greatest charms is the family's portraits, furniture and belongings, which have been gathered across four centuries. There is a sense of continuity, warmth and pride in the presentation of the Palmer family home.

As in all real homes, not everything was always sweetness and light. The first of the Palmers at Dorney Court had warned his son Roger about marrying the beautiful Barbara Villiers. The young man ignored the advice that he would be made utterly miserable and went ahead. Barbara continued her affair with Lord Chesterfield and then became Charles II's favourite mistress. Roger ran away to serve in the navy.

The first pineapple grown in England was produced by Dorney Court's gardener in 1665: the King got the fruit, too, and a painting commemorating the occasion is displayed at the house.

Easter, Fri–Mon; May, Suns and BH; Jun–Sept, Sun–Tue; all 2–5.30pm. Tel: 0628 604638.

FAWLEY COURT ★★
Map p.140, C4
1 mile N of Henley off the A4155

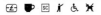

Fawley Court has a lingering atmosphere of authentic age. Never excessively restored, it has retained a profound feeling of reality: everything is slightly makeshift, slightly down-at-heel, cracked here, faded there. There are no period reconstructions or set pieces; instead, it has precisely the feel an old house should have: as if the occupants have only just moved out.

There has been a house on this spot for over a thousand years. First the manor of a Saxon earl, it was given after the Norman Conquest to William I's brother-in-law, Walter Gifford, a compiler of the Domesday Book. In 1079 it came into the hands of Sir William de Sakeville, whose family, the Sackvilles, lived there for almost 400 years. The fortified castle that they built in the 12th century was demolished by Royalist artillery in the Civil War.

In 1684 the estate's new owner, Colonel William Freeman, commissioned his friend Christopher Wren to build him a family home and the result, much as it stands today, was Fawley Court. The Ionic colonnade was added by James Wyatt in the late 18th century when various changes were made to the outside. The interior, which was restored in 1974 following fire damage, includes a splendid 17th-century plasterwork ceiling in the saloon, executed by Grinling Gibbons. There are late 18th-century stucco decorations in the library and several good fireplaces.

The surrounding parkland, laid out by Capability Brown in 1771, has been much altered. There are several follies, including a 'ruin' with a domed room, a dairy and watergate. The park actually straddles three counties, since the Island Temple, designed by Wyatt in 1771 is in Berkshire and the gardens extend, upstream, into Oxfordshire.

The house was requisitioned for wartime service by British Military Intelligence, but by 1953 it had fallen into decline. It was purchased by the Polish Congregation of Marian Fathers, and until 1986 it housed the Divine Mercy boarding school for boys. Fawley Court is now a religious retreat.

Much has been done to refurbish the interior and a some of the rooms are now open to the public. These contain a number of relics relating to Polish history – predominantly martial but with some incongruous touches such as a collection of 3rd-century Roman coins and a copy of

Petronius's pornographic *Satyricon*. Visitors are free to roam the grounds.
Mar–Oct, Wed, Thur, Sun 2–5pm except Easter and Whitsun. Sat: parties by arrangment.
Tel: 0491 574917.

HUGHENDEN MANOR ★ ★
Map p.146, E2
1 mile N of High Wycombe on the A4128

☒ ☒ ⚔ ♿ *(gd floor & terrace)* ♨ ✕

Set splendidly on the spur of a ridge separating two steep-sided valleys, the house is surrounded by a large park and terraced gardens that command panoramic views towards High Wycombe. Built in the mid-18th century, it was acquired by the National Trust in 1946. Its present appearance is the result of major remodelling in 1862 by the architect E.B.Lamb for Benjamin Disraeli, who acquired the property in 1848 and lived in the house during both his terms as Prime Minister, in 1868 and from 1874–80.

The design was intended to convey a Jacobean flavour, with angular, red brickwork, battlemented roof line and pinnacles. The 18th-century plaster ceiling and fireplace in the library are all that remain of the earlier interior. The Jacobean influence can best be seen in the ribbed ceilings that occur throughout most of the house, even in the smallest rooms. The old library, now the Drawing Room, has diamond patterned ribbing on its ceiling, a twin arch dividing the room and Gothic furnishings which give it a distinctively Victorian character. The Gothic theme is continued in the Dining Room, where a portrait of Queen Victoria hangs. The house contains a large collection of objects associated with Disraeli and his family and his study remains much as it must have looked on his death in 1881 (picture, p.36).

St Michael and All Angels Church and its churchyard are situated in the park, surrounded by grazing livestock, on sloping ground on the approach to the house. Disraeli was buried in a vault beneath the north chapel and a white marble memorial to him was erected there by Queen Victoria.

Mar, Sat & Sun 2–6pm. Apr–Oct, Wed–Sat 2–6pm; Sun & BH Mon 12–6pm. Closed Good Fri. Tel: 0494 532580.

MENTMORE TOWERS ★ ★
Map p150, D3
3 miles NW of Ivinghoe off the B488

☒ ♟ ⚔ ♿ ✕

Rising from the surrounding woodland, the Towers are visible for miles. The house was built for Baron Meyer de Rothschild in 1855 by the architects Sir Joseph Paxton, the designer of London's Crystal Palace, and his son-in-law G. H. Stokes. Made from Ancaster stone with a wealth of Jacobean detail, it was created as a pastiche of the Elizabethan Woollaton Hall in Nottingham. The house was the first of its size to have central heating and hot running water, and at one time it had the largest glass doors in Europe. These opened into the Great Hall – 45 ft long by 36 ft wide and more than 30 ft high, with complex ridged glazing on its roof.

Like other members of his family, Baron Rothschild was a great collector. He filled the Towers with an enormous collection of French furniture, porcelain and *objets d'art*, and even had a marble chimney piece brought to Mentmore from the Rubens house in Antwerp. In 1878, his only child married the fifth Earl of Rosebery (later to become Prime Minister), and the house passed to the Rosebery family. During the earl's occupancy, the house played host to guests such as Napoleon III, Gladstone, Disraeli and Czar Nicholas II of Russia. Several members of the British royal family planted trees in the spacious grounds.

Mentmore came down through several generations of the Rosebery family, but in 1978, exactly 100 years after the first Rosebery moved in, the Towers had to be sold to raise money for death duties. Although the house and everything that went with it were offered to the government at a price of £6 million, the offer was turned down, prompting the auctioning of the contents in what the press of the time called 'the sale of the century'.

The house itself went for a song – £240,000 – to the Maharishi University of

Natural Law, headed by the Indian guru Mararishi Mahesh Yogi. His followers, who teach transcendental meditation and practise 'yogic flying', have since used the house as a training and research centre. The house and grounds are open to the public on Sundays and Bank Holidays, and it is let out for craft fairs, open air classical concerts and the filming of pop videos.

Although much of its interior grandeur disappeared in the auction, the Towers is still worth seeing for its sheer immensity. The Five Arrows, the mark of the Rothschild family representing the five sons who left to form banking houses in different European capitals, can still be seen – for instance in the window surrounds of the Gold Room, which is lined with gold silk wall hangings.
Suns & BH. Hours vary. Tel: 0296 661881.

NETHER WINCHENDON HOUSE ★
Map p.149, F1
½ mile N of Cuddington on minor roads off the A418

Built in 1533, Nether Winchendon House was originally part of the Notley Abbey estate, near Haddenham, but was given to the first Earl of Bedford after the Dissolution in 1547. Since the 18th century it has been the home of the Spencer-Bernard family, the first being Sir Francis Bernard, sometime governor of New Jersey and Massachusetts, who lived there until his death in 1780.

Originally a Tudor and medieval timber-framed house, it has been much added to, most notably by a Gothic screen around the courtyard. But an ancient avenue of lime trees still leads the way to the front entrance and the magnificent Tudor chimneys are still prominent. The house was restored in 1958 and the gardens replanted. Inside there is a large collection of tapestries and family portraits.

The Spencer-Bernards allow the village fete to take place in the grounds and visitors are free to look around during part of the summer.
May, every day 2.30–5.30pm and Aug BH. Other times by app. Tel: 0844 290101.

STOWE LANDSCAPE GARDENS ★ ★ ★
Map p.152, E3
Two miles N of Buckingham off the A422

'The faire majestic paradise of Stowe' has been showered with praise since work began on the 250-acre landscape gardens in the early 18th century; with six lakes and 32 surviving garden temples, they have been described as one of the supreme creations of the Georgian era, the most important landscape gardens in Britain and the biggest work of art in the land.

The gardens were initially the dream of one man, Sir Richard Temple, later Viscount Cobham; one of Marlborough's generals, he used a period in the political wilderness to devote himself to making Stowe the finest house in England. Work began in 1713; in 1730, Cobham engaged the great English garden architect William Kent to create one of the first 'natural' landscapes, in fact a triumph of artifice in which carefully asymmetrical patterns were allowed to blend with the surrounding countryside. With James Gibbs, Kent built tree-lined avenues, streams, and valleys and graced them with a whole range of bridges, temples and columns, with much associated statuary and all in an elegant classical style.

Cobham died in 1749, but his heir and nephew Earl Temple continued his dream. Lancelot 'Capability' Brown, who was head gardener for the ten years following 1741, added lakes and woodland; Earl Temple personally designed, with some professional guidance, the Grecian Temple and the Temples of Concord and Victory. He commissioned Robert Adam to draw up plans for the south front of the house in 1770, and the Grand Avenue was laid out in the same year. By the end of the

The Octagon Pond, Stowe Gardens

century the landscaping was mostly completed, much as it remains today.

But Stowe's golden age was ending rapidly. By the mid-19th century, the income from the estate was not enough for Temple's heir, the free-spending and debt-ridden second Duke of Buckingham and Chandos. In 1848, he avoided bankruptcy only by selling 36,000 acres, the entire contents of the house and thousands of trees. In 1921 the whole estate was sold off, and for a time it looked as if the great house might be demolished. Instead, Stowe public school was founded, and it acquired a new life as a working building.

The gardens came under the care of the National Trust in 1989, thanks to a benefactor who still remains anonymous, and since then the Trust and its volunteer helpers have been tireless in their restoration work, ranging from the dredging of rivers and lakes to the delicate refurbishment of the monuments. Much remains to be done, but Stowe's gardens are still overwhelmingly magnificent.

A full day, or at the very least an afternoon, is needed to do justice to all they have to offer, for the route through the park takes two hours to walk briskly, beginning with at the great Corinthian arch that frames the entrance to Earl Temple's avenue. In summer, visits can be evening occasions; there is usually an annual opera festival and a full-scale outdoor orchestral concert with a fireworks display.

The house itself is still the home of Stowe School; it is open to the public only at certain times in the year.
Gardens: Most days 10am–5pm or dusk. Open days vary according to school calendar. Open every day during vacations, in term time, Mon, Wed, Fri, Sun. Tel: 0280 822850.
House: (not NT). Easter–Oct: selected days in school vacation. Tel: 0280 813164.

WADDESDON MANOR ★ ★
Map p.149, E1
5 miles NW of Aylesbury off the A41

♿ 💼 🆂🅲 🧒 ♿ 🥾 ✈

Baron Ferdinand de Rothschild first came to Waddesdon for the hunting, and liked

it so much that he decided to build an enormous, Loire-style chateau on the top of Lodge Hill as his home. He acquired the land in 1874 from the Duke of Marlborough and set the architect Gabriel-Hippolyte Destailleur to work on what was to be one of the most spectacular country houses built in the 19th century (picture, p.115).

No expense was spared. A team of Percheron mares was brought from Normandy to drag the Bath stone across country for the house. The top of the hill was flattened and the Duke of Buckingham's tramway from Quainton Road was extended to serve the manor's grounds. And as it took shape Waddesdon Manor became one of the unrivalled visiting places of the literary and political elite of England.Queen Victoria herself arrived by steam train, amid much pomp and ceremony, to see the place with her own eyes in 1890.

The east wing was completed in 1880, and the rest of the manor was finished by 1893, a turreted spectacle visible for miles around. The grounds were landscaped by the French architect Laine to include a long, winding drive set amid trees. Statues include a copy of the Apollo Belvedere in the Vatican – and its fountain pool.

The contents of the house include a wealth of 18th-century French carved wood panelling, Savonnerie carpets, Sèvres porcelain, French 17th- and 18th-century furniture and a collection of arms and armour through the ages. There are paintings by French, Italian and Dutch masters, as well as works by Gainsborough, Reynolds and Romney.

James de Rothschild gave Waddesdon Manor and the grounds to the National Trust in 1957 and some of the contents went to the British Museum. The manor closed for extensive refurbishment in 1989 and is not expected to re-open until 1994. The National Trust is currently installing Louis XV panelling bought by Baron Ferdinand but never shown before to the public and is planning a series of six monthly rotating exhibitions relating to the Rothschild family history and their interest in architecture, music and the arts.

Meanwhile the grounds, with aviary,

and part of the house are open to a limited degree for variable hours.

Batchelor Wing & Wine Cellar: *Apr–mid-Oct.*
Gardens, Aviary, Shop, Tearoom: *Apr–Dec.*
Waddesdon Manor Estate Office.
Tel: 0296 651282.

WEST WYCOMBE PARK ★ ★ ★
Map p.146, F1
2 miles NW of High Wycombe off the A40

£ & *(grounds only)* ✗

The original West Wycombe Park was built between 1710-15, following the acquisition of the estate in 1698, together with the village of West Wycombe, by Francis Dashwood, a London merchant who had made his fortune in the silk trade. The present house, however, with its landscaped park, is the inspired creation of his son, Sir Francis Dashwood, who inherited the property in 1724 at the age of sixteen (picture, p.123).

The transformation of house and park, which was begun in 1735 and continued, with the involvement of several different architects, until Sir Francis's death in 1781, clearly reflects the influence of a series of Grand Tours he made across Europe. The 1775 two-tiered colonnade with columns of plastered wood, for example, which dominates the south front, is derived from Palladio's Palazzo Chiericati in Vicenza, while the Ionic portico on the west front is based on drawings of the Temple of Bacchus at Teos.

The interiors display a sumptuous elegance throughout. Particularly impressive are the Hall and Dining Room, with their patterned floors, marbled walls, elaborately decorated ceilings and rich furnishings. The Tapestry Room, Red and Blue Drawing Rooms all have fine painted ceilings, the latter depicting Bacchus, the God of Wine, as befitted its 18th-century role as a dining room. The Music Room is perhaps the grandest of all, with a painted ceiling based on Raphael's 'Banquet of the Gods' at the Villa Farnesina, and a chimneypiece that is the most elaborate in the house. The Saloon, which displays pictures brought back from the Grand Tour and has a ceiling representing the 'Council of the Gods', has a superb view over the park to the church and mausoleum on the hill.

The park is one of the finest 18th-century landscaped gardens in the country. Its central feature is the great lake in which, on the largest of three islands, the Temple of Music stands reflected in still waters. To the west of the lake is the Broadwalk, flanked by woods with serpentine streams and meandering paths which connect the many temples and follies dotted around the park. The Temple of Venus, which sits on a mound in a clearing in the woods, with a small grotto beneath, is a replacement for the original temple that was contemporary with the earliest alterations to the house. The Temple of the Winds, which stands at the east end of the ha-ha, was once more prominent as it aligned with an earlier approach to the house, along a drive that entered the park between the twin gatehouses of Daphne's Temple and Kitty's Lodge. The lake is dammed on the east side by the Cascade, at one end of a long canal, but the river does not leave the estate until it reaches the Pepperpot Bridge on the Marlow road. The house and its grounds were given to the National Trust in 1943.

Grounds only: *Apr & May, Sun & Wed 2–6pm; Easter, May & Spring BH Sun & Mon 2–6pm.*
House and grounds: *June–Aug, Sun–Thur 2–6pm. Tel: 0494 524411.*

BLACK PARK & LANGLEY PARK COUNTRY PARKS ★
Map p.142, C4
2 miles NE of Slough off the A412

 ♥ 🏹 *(by arrangement)* ♿ 🔋 ℹ️

A huge range of outdoor pursuits is available in these twin country parks, situated on opposite sides of the main road in pleasant countryside with a good balance between woodland and open space. In Black Park to the north of the A412 the fittest might try the orienteering course, canoeing and swimming in the lake; model boating and fishing are also available for the less strenuously inclined.

Langley Country Park, across the road to the south, has a designated campsite (without facilities) and an arboretum. Both parks are easily large enough to satisfy walkers, cyclists and horse riders looking for countryside to explore safely without travelling too far from urban areas; motorway access is close, and both attract considerable numbers of school parties. *All year, 8am–dusk. Tel: (Rangers' Office, Black Park) 0753 511060.*

BUCKS GOAT CENTRE, LAYBY FARM ★
Map p.146, A1
½ mile S of Stoke Mandeville off the A4010

 💷 ♥ 🆂🅲 ♿

Owners Michael and Julia Gaisford have turned their farm into a specialist mini-zoo that features every breed of goat in the country as well as sheep, poultry, ponies, rabbits, guinea pigs and other small animals. Open all year round, the centre is popular with children and adults alike, and bags of fodder are available for hands-on feeding of the animals.

The Gaisfords run a successful autumn goat-mating programme and travel throughout Europe to find the right goats to breed with their existing stock. Those they do not want to keep are often available for sale to purchasers with large gardens or farms.

The information centre has facilities for talks and seminars and school and other parties are welcome by appointment. Also on the site is a farm shop selling crafts, gifts souvenirs and farm produce, a café, a pine and cane furniture shop and a garden nursery.

There are pony rides at the weekends and tastings of goats' cheese and other farm produce throughout the week. *All year, Tue-Sun 10am–4.30pm. Tel: 0296 612983.*

CHILTERN OPEN AIR MUSEUM ★ ★
Map p.147, F2
1 mile E of Chalfont St Giles off the A413

 💷 ♥ 🆂🅲 🏹 *(by arrangement)* ✈

The theme of the museum, founded in 1976, is 'Buildings Through the Ages'. Sited in about 45 acres of attractive park and woodland once belonging to the adjacent Newland Park (now a college), it houses a wide variety of historic buildings of relevance to the Chilterns, many of which would have been lost forever had they not been carefully dismantled and then re-erected within the museum. Only once an irrevocable decision to demolish has been taken will the museum consider taking any particular building: its general policy is that structures of historic interest should be left on their original sites, if possible.

The museum is in constant development, and additions are continually made to its stock. Apart from one reproduction iron-age house, every building was once sited somewhere within the Chilterns area, and the museum guide book has details of precise origins. Exhibits range from a traditional red, GPO telephone kiosk and an Edwardian public convenience (still in use for the comfort of visitors – and regional winner of the 1991 'Loo of the Year Award'), through a variety of farm buildings, to a former High Wycombe furniture factory, a 1940s prefab, and a brick-built toll house.

The museum ticket office at the main gate is itself an old pavilion and houses a craft and materials exhibition of relevance to the museum, while the ground floor of the furniture factory now sells refreshments. There is a specially-constructed nature trail within the site and also a children's playground.

Throughout the season, the museum runs a number of one-off, special event days on various themes. School parties are welcome.
Apr–Oct, Weds–Sun & BH Mons, 2–6pm. Tel: 0494 871117.

DENHAM COUNTRY PARK ★
Map p.143, B1
1 mile E of Denham off the A412

P *(seasonal)* ✗ *(for events)* ♿ ☕

Still and running water are the main features of the park. The Grand Union Canal, three rivers – the Misbourne, the Frays and the Colne – a series of ponds, together with water meadow and woodland provide habitats for a variety of wildlife; its wetland offers increasingly scarce sanctuary for newts and frogs, among other creatures.

The park is L-shaped, about a mile and a half long but only a few hundred yards wide in some places. Its rangers conduct guided rambles (by appointment) to help extract the greatest value from a visit, and special events are frequently organized. Arrangements can be made for school trips.
All year, 8.30am–dusk.
Visitors' Centre: *Summer, 8.30am–6pm; Winter, 8.30am–5pm. Tel: 0895 835852.*

EMBERTON COUNTRY PARK ★
Map p.156, F2
1 mile S of Olney off the A509

£ P SC ♿ ☕ ℹ

With a mile of river frontage onto the Great Ouse, and incorporating four lakes within its 170 acres, Emberton Country Park provides for a wide range of outdoor activities. There is fishing, boating and sailing as well as putting, pitch-and-putt and picnic facilities for campers, caravanners and day-trippers alike. A wide range of equipment, from boats and bicycles to life-jackets and putting clubs, can be hired on-site, as can picnic chairs, trestle tables and even gas barbecues. National River Authority fishing licences are also available. All items for sale or hire can be obtained from the Information Centre near the Tea Rooms. For further information apply to the Gate House.

This award-winning park, which also includes a children's nature trail and a climbing crag (for certificated climbers only), is a fine example of land reclamation following the damage caused by gravel quarrying during construction of the nearby M1 motorway. Emberton Park is owned and managed by Milton Keynes Borough Council.
Every day. Apr–Oct, 9am–6pm; Nov–Mar, 9.30am–3pm. Tel: 0234 713325.

FLAMINGO GARDENS AND ZOOLOGICAL PARK ★ ★
Map p.156, F2
1 mile SW of Olney off the A509

£ SC ✗ *(by arrangement)* ♿ ✈

Just east of the village of Weston Underwood, on the road to Olney, the Flamingo Gardens and Zoological Park house one of the finest collections of rare birds anywhere in Britain, including the only American Bald Eagles to be bred in captivity in the UK.

The park was founded 30 years ago by the present owner, Mr Christopher Marler, to collect and breed the world's rarer birds, especially those threatened with extinction through the greed and ignorance of man. His tally now includes a gamut of birdlife ranging from the Caribbean Flamingo and the Carolina Duck, to African Yellow-Billed Storks, Arctic Bewick Swans, and the Milky Stork from Sumatra. In all, about 150 species of bird – and a few mammal species too – comprise the current collection.

The gardens enclose a three-acre shrubbery known as 'the Wilderness', roamed by peacocks and cranes, where two

centuries ago the poet William Cowper wrote some of his famous lines. Cowper's verse can be found inscribed on statues and pedestals throughout the Flamingo Gardens.
2–7.00pm: Mar–Jun and Sept, Wed, Thu, Sat, Sun and BH; Jul–Aug, every day except Mon. Tel: 0234 711451.

THE HOME OF REST FOR HORSES *
Map p.146, D1
3 miles SE of Princes Risborough off the A4010, nr Lacey Green

&

The Home of Rest for Horses, Mules and Donkeys, as it was originally called, was established by Ann Lindo in 1886 to provide a retreat for working horses on the streets of London. It originally occupied a field at Neasden, but soon needed to move to larger premises, first to stables at Acton, then in 1908 to Cricklewood, where it stayed until 1934. Its next home was at Boreham Wood until 1971, when it moved to its present location at Speen Farm in the Chiltern Hills.

Its success in the early years was due in part to the patronage of the Duke of Portland, Master of the Royal Household; it has always been run entirely on charitable donations. The Home worked closely with the Royal Veterinary College in the 1930s and gained a reputation as the best facility of its kind in the world.

The present stables have about 100 animals in residence each day during the summer months and about 120 in the winter. Altogether, about 200 horses, ponies and donkeys pass through the stables each year, some for short stays, and others for life, like Sefton, retired from the Household Cavalry. Visitors who wish to feed the animals should bring their own carrots.

You can combine a visit with walks in the area from Great Hampden or Bradenham, and there is a footpath to the Home from Lacey Green mill (see p.29).

All year: (except last Thu in Jul & Xmas Day) 2–4pm. All children must be accompanied by an adult. Tel: 0494 488464.

RARE BREEDS CENTRE ★ ★
Map p.142, B2
2 ½ miles S of Beaconsfield on minor roads

£ ● SC ✕

The Rare Breeds Centre, between Wooburn Green and Littleworth Common, is on the 140-acre Odds Farm, itself home to a traditional breed of beef cattle. The Centre has been created to protect some of the older and rarer kinds of British farm animals that would otherwise be in danger of extinction. These include the Tamworth pig, Castlemilk Moorit and Wiltshire Horn sheep, British White and Highland cattle, and the Golden Guernsey goat. All told, there are 45 different breeds of animals and fowl on display, some of which are reduced to less than 200 breeding females worldwide. All have been farmed at some time but are no longer commercially viable. The Centre not only maintains a pedigree breeding stock, but provides less exotic farm animals for cross breeding.

The Centre is set out with children in mind, providing the opportunity for them to observe the animals closely in a series of paddocks and covered outbuildings. They can compare old and new breeds and learn about feeding methods, and animal life-cycles as well as the history of some of the rarer breeds. The breeding season is spread over five months of the year, so there are new arrivals to see from spring until the end of summer. Lambing is from April to May, while goats are kidding from May to June, cows calving from June to July, and pigs farrowing throughout the year. There is also a pets' corner where children can handle the animals, including rabbits and guinea pigs, and special food is available for feeding. There are likely to be school parties visiting on most weekday mornings.
Daily: Apr–Oct, 10am–5pm. Tel: 0628 520188.

DAYS OUT *Special Interest*

BEKONSCOT MODEL VILLAGE ★ ★
Map p.142, A2
Warwick Rd, Beaconsfield, just N of station

⌷ ▼ SC ⌷ ⌷ ✕

Much of Beaconsfield may be new, but amidst the Metroland sprawl lies an astonishing piece of modern antiquity: the 40,000 square ft of Bekonscot, the oldest model village in the world and a time capsule that has thrilled children and adults alike since it first opened in 1929. Started as a hobby by London accountant Roland Callingham, Bekonscot has expanded over the decades into a microcosm of 1930s English life (picture, p.31).

There is something of everything here – castle, church, cathedral, village, zoo, windmill, amusement pier and fairground. Bekonscot has its own cricket pitch, flying club and race track, its own golf course, beach and bowling green. It even boasts its own working coal mine. Meanwhile, the whole community is served by 438 yards of miniature railway track.

Much of Bekonscot is based on original, real-life architecture such as Sydney Harbour Bridge, Hampton Court Maze, Eton College and a number of local Beaconsfield buildings. Great attention has been paid to detail, and walking along the village's smooth – full-size – paths it is possible to make out individual shop signs and advertisements.

As much care is taken over the landscape as the models themselves. Two hundred tons of stone were used for the rockeries alone, and the trees, shrubs and flowers, which are carefully selected to blend in with the scale of the village, make a blaze of summer colour. There are miniature willows, lilacs and roses, Japanese bonsai trees, and even some specimens that thrive ready-stunted in the wilds of Finland.

Bekonscot has always operated on a charitable basis, with all surplus profits going to worthy causes. Since 1929 the village has distributed well in excess of three million pounds, and from 1978 it has been run directly by the Church Army, who continue to channel the money to where it is most needed.

A souvenir shop and first-aid room can be found in the converted railway carriage which forms the ticket office. For those who become bored with miniature entertainment there is also a picnic ground and a spacious play area.
Daily, Mid Feb–Oct, 10am–5pm. Tel: 0494 672919.

BUCKINGHAMSHIRE RAILWAY CENTRE ★ ★
Map p.149, D1
1 mile S of Quainton off the A41

⌷ ▼ SC ✗ *(parties by arrangement)* ⌷ ✕

With a real railway station at its heart, the Buckinghamshire Railway Centre is a haven for railway enthusiasts. Quainton Road station was on the Duke of Buckingham's private tramway (closed in the 1930s) before it became the meeting point of the Great Central and Metropolitan lines from London to Manchester. Now the tracks in front of the station's platforms are quiet, except for the occasional rubbish-laden train bound for the Calvert landfill site to the north-east.

However, over the years the station has become home to a collection of locomotives, carriages and wagons from Britain's mainline and suburban railways throughout the ages of steam and diesel, together with examples from South Africa, America and Egypt. The centre is staffed by volunteers, and is open at weekends throughout the year for visitors to see the platforms, footbridge, ticket office, signal box and other working parts of yesteryear's stations.

They can also admire the collection of rolling stock, including the centre's splendid old dining car from the London and North-Western Railway, once part of the Royal train and now hired out for special functions. Appropriately, a New

York subway carriage has been converted to form the centre's café.

On viewing days, the centre's museum, gift shop and refreshment coach are open but locomotives are not usually in steam; on steaming days, an engine is kept with steam up and the centre's own miniature railway is running. There are regular visits by Thomas the Tank Engine and in the weeks up to Christmas Santa and his helpers take their own train round the track and hand out presents to the children on board.

Grown-ups who want to realise their childhood ambitions can sign up for the centre's half-day steam train driving courses and schools, by prior appointment, can be given guided tours with ready-prepared notes thrown in. The centre is also available as a venue for club and society outings.

Every day, not necessarily with all or any facilities. Tel: 0296 655720.

Viewing days: *Apr–Oct, Sats, 10am–4pm.*

Steaming days: *Apr–Oct, Suns & BH, 11am–6pm; Jun–Aug & Oct half term, also Weds, 11am–6pm.*

CHILTERN BREWERY, TERRICK
Map p.146, A2 ★ ★

1 mile N of Wendover off the A413

£ ♟ SC ✗ *(no other tours)* ⅙ ✕

Richard and Lesley Jenkinson set up their brewery in 1980 with the aim of producing high quality, traditionally-brewed English beers with a local flavour, and visitors can see the workings of the business for themselves. Their small-is-beautiful approach has so far produced the light Chiltern Ale, Beechwood Bitter, Three Hundreds Old Ale and the brainstorming Bodgers Barley Wine (a very strong bottle-conditioned ale sold in half pints). Available in selected pubs throughout the area, all these are on sale in the brewery shop as well as a range of mustards, chutneys, cakes, cheeses and preserves, all made with beer.

Richard Jenkinson personally takes parties on two types of tour around the brewery – the 'Tippler's' and the 'Drayman's'.

On the two-hour Tippler's tour, group parties (a minimum of 12) are given beer samples and an introductory talk before being shown around the brewery. All processes are explained on the way, with stops that include the malt store where the milling, mashing, and boiling of the ingredients takes place and the hop store where the beers are fermented, conditioned and finally bottled and casked. At the end there is more sampling and a chance for discussion.

The Drayman's tour is identical, but ends in a self-service buffet that includes a choice of the brewery's cheeses and hop-pickled onions.

The shop contains the Jenkinsons' collection of brewing memorabilia: a solid oak sampling bench, a Customs and Excise desk and a sampling cellar stillion, rescued from a brewery closed in 1988. Beer can be ordered in advance in 36 pint polypins, 72 pint firkins and 144 pint kilderkins – ready to be picked up at the end of the tour.

Shop: *Mon–Sat, 9am–5pm.*

Brewery: *by appointment. Tel: 0296 613647.*

JOHN MILTON'S COTTAGE MUSEUM ★ ★
Map p.147, F2

1 mile N of Gerrards Cross on the A413

£

Set on Chalfont St Giles High St, this 16th-century cottage is the only surviving building in which the poet John Milton (1608–1674) is known to have lived. It was very nearly demolished brick-by-brick to be re-erected in the USA, but was saved for the nation in 1887 by a public subscription to which Queen Victoria personally donated a regal £20. To commemorate the centenary of the appeal, Queen Elizabeth II visited the museum in 1987.

Milton came to Chalfont St Giles in 1665 to escape the great plague then raging in London. His friend and former pupil, Thomas Ellwood, then living nearby, found the cottage for him and persuaded him to complete his magnum opus, *Paradise Lost*, begun in 1642, and subsequently to write *Paradise Regained*.

Milton had been active in the cause of

the Parliamentarians, and was for some time Latin secretary to Cromwell. By 1665, however, with the monarchy back in power, he was living in much reduced circumstances and in fear of imprisonment. To add further to his woes, he was already blind by the time of his arrival in Chalfont St Giles, and wrote his great works by dictating late into the night to his daughter, working by candle-light.

The museum comprises two public rooms within the cottage, which house a number of relics, artefacts and objects of local interest contemporary with Milton. There are first editions of *Paradise Lost* and *Paradise Regained*, together with a small library of his other works, including various limited editions and translations. The museum furniture includes a pair of fine Cromwellian chairs. Other Cromwellian relics include cannon-balls found embedded in St Giles's church a few hundred yards away. Visitors are also free to wander the small garden, which has a well and an ancient vine.
Mar–Oct, weekdays 10am–1pm, 2–6pm; Suns 2–6pm, Spring & Summer BH
Tel: 0494 872313.

LACEY GREEN WINDMILL ★★
Map p.145, D4
3 miles SE of Princes Risborough off the A4010
£

Sited at the north end of Lacey Green, the highest village in the Chilterns, Lacey Green Windmill is the oldest of its kind in the country. A smock mill – so called because its shape resembles the smocks once worn by farm labourers – it was built in 1650 and originally stood at CHESHAM, more than 8 miles from its present position, to which it was moved in 1821. Such a major undertaking was not as bizarre then as it might appear today. As one of the most advanced power sources of their day, mills were valued items of equipment and downland farmers saw nothing strange in carting them to new and windier positions. Many were transported whole, but in Lacey Green's case the mill probably had to be dismantled for a complete overhaul – by 1821 it was over

170 years old – which would have considerably simplified the journey. At about the same time, the owners equipped it with a set of patent sails and a fantail.

The mill tower comprises a weatherboarded timber frame, which sits on a brick plinth, the upper part of the cellar wall. The revolving cap, which overhangs the tower, has a steep, curving roof that resembles the keel of an upturned boat. The fantail was fitted on the back of the cap and ensured that the main sails would always be turned into the wind, while the patent sails themselves had wooden shutters that could be adjusted by the miller to alter their set without stopping the mill.

The internal machinery still retains many features from the original mill. And in its later form at least, it was a highly sophisticated device that could adapt to variations in windspeed or adjust the fineness of the flour, yet required only one person to operate it.

The mill was in use until 1915. Subsequently, its condition deteriorated, although repairs in the 1930s prevented total collapse. During World War II, it served as a watch tower for the Home Guard, and later became a farm store, before it again fell into disrepair. The task of restoration was begun in 1967 by the Chiltern Society and continued over the next 20 years. It is now in full working order.
May–Sept, Sun & BH Mon 2.30–5.30pm.
Tel: 0844 343560.

WEST WYCOMBE CAVES ★
Map p.146, F1
2 miles NW of High Wycombe off the A40
£ 🏴 SC ✕

In 1750 Sir Francis Dashwood, creator of West Wycombe Park (see p.23), decided to provide work for the area following a succession of disastrous harvests. Quarrying started in the chalk hillside above West Wycombe, to provide material for a road to High Wycombe. Two years later High Wycombe had its new road and Dashwood had a new feature in his landscaped realm: a labyrinth of caves,

29

extending ¼ mile into the hill, which would soon become notorious as the meeting-place of the Hell-Fire Club, a semi-secret society of aristocratic rakehells founded by Dashwood.

The club disbanded in 1763, principally through political rivalry during a period when Dashwood was an unsuccessful Chancellor of the Exchequer. But there were other reasons: even by 18th-century standards, its members' blasphemous and libertine behaviour was considered too scandalous to continue.

The caves are entered through a large, flint courtyard resembling the interior of a ruined, Gothic church, and the names given to their various chambers – the Robing Room, the Catacombs, the Banqueting Hall, the Monks' Cells, the River Styx, the Cursing Well and the Inner Temple – all serve to evoke the pagan (and highly indecent) rituals that were rumoured to have taken place.

Electric lighting was installed in the 1950s, when the caves were opened to the public by the Dashwood family. But the long, winding tunnels still retain a chilly eeriness that is best experienced without the company of other visitors.
Mid Mar–Sept, 11am–6pm. Oct–Mar, Sat & Sun 1–5pm. Tel: 0494 524411.

WYCOMBE AIR PARK ★ ★
Map p.141, A2
3 miles NW of Marlow off the B482

⊞ 🆂🅲 𝅅 *(parties by arrangement)* ♿ ✕

Wycombe Air Park, which began by collecting parts from crashed wartime aeroplanes, has restored and rebuilt vintage aircraft at Booker, south-west of High Wycombe, since the early 1970s. There are machines dating from 1909 onwards, of which 15 are still flown, and during the summer months some of these may be seen in practice over the airfield. Far from being pensioned off as nostalgic curiosities, they now earn their keep as movie stand-ins – many aerial sequences are shot at Booker.

The museum also has displays to explain how special effects are created using radio-controlled models and there is a collection of film memorabilia.
Apr–Oct and on special occasions, 10am–5pm. Tel: 0494 529432.

WYCOMBE LOCAL HISTORY & CHAIR MUSEUM ★
Map p.146, F2
Castle Hill House, Priory Avenue, High Wycombe

🆂🅲 𝅅 ✕

Contained within and around an 18th-century, flint-faced house, this small museum explores the history of High Wycombe and the crafts that made it wealthy, concentrating especially on chair-making, the industry which dominated the area during the 18th and 19th centuries.

In 1798, the parish of Wycombe held some fifty chair-makers, mostly small family concerns. With the advent of mass-production, however, the industry diversified and expanded at an astonishing rate. By 1870, with output standing at a staggering 5,000 chairs per day, the town was being heralded as 'the furniture capital of England' – a title made manifest on royal visits, when a mighty arch of chairs was built across the High Street between the Guildhall and the houses opposite.

The old stables behind the museum include a reconstructed Framer's Workshop, a typical example of those that existed in Wycombe during the late 19th century; it contains the tools belonging to Jack Goodchild, one of the leading makers of the Windsor Chair, which first appeared in 1732. A separate room in the house is devoted to the history of its manufacture.

The museum, naturally, houses a fine collection of chairs. But this is not all. Other featured crafts include lace-making, straw plait and rush work, paper-making and ploughing.
All year, Mon–Fri, 10am–5pm; Sat, 10am–1pm & 2–5pm. Tel: 0494 421895.

Bekonscot Model Village, Beaconsfield

A–Z of Towns and Villages

ADDINGTON

Map p.149, B1
2 miles NW of Winslow off the A413

Set at the end of an unmetalled track off the lane from the main road, the tiny, secluded hamlet of Addington has two imposing houses. Visitors heading for the church will first come to an imposing neo-Georgian home built in the 1920s. The track then bears to the right towards the original manor house, set in parkland and dating from the 17th century.

St Mary's Church has a 14th-century tower and arcades. Its windows include a series of fine Flemish stained glass panels. The church also had an Italian sketch of the baroque period, but it was stolen in the 1970s. In earlier times, the church's guardians were driven to extreme measures to protect its valuables. In the 16th century, when Henry VIII ordered the destruction of Catholic books, its library was walled up so carefully that the treasures remained undiscovered until the church was much rebuilt 300 years later. The books are now in a secure display.

As a boy the actor Laurence Olivier sang in the church choir: his father was the vicar. Later, during World War II, the conductor Malcolm Sargent lived in a local cottage and sometimes played the church organ.

ADSTOCK

Map p.149, A1
3 miles NW of Winslow off the A413

Adstock is a small, peaceful village surrounded by farm land a few hundred yards north-east of the main road. Although most of its buildings are modern or Victorian, it still has a number of thatched and timber-framed houses and the village pub, The Old Thatched Inn, lives up to its name.

St Cecilia's Church has some Norman features retained despite extensive rebuilding and refurbishment through the centuries. The west tower is topped by battlements. The stained glass in the west window is Victorian.

AKELEY

Map p.152, E4
3 miles N of Buckingham on the A413

Akeley is built around a winding hill on the main road. Like most similar settlements, it was once a self-sufficient community complete with shops, inns, a pottery, a slaughter house and a coffin maker; unlike many today, it retains at least a school and one surviving pub, the Bull and Butcher,

But it no longer has a church: Akeley's former St James's Church was declared redundant and unsafe, and demolished in 1979. Akeley's people were disgusted: there had been a church in the village since the 12th century.

The **Bull and Butcher**, in the square opposite the church site, demonstrates the kind of initiative that small businesses in small places need to survive: the landlady has a sideline as an acupuncturist.

AMERSHAM

Map p.147, E1
7 miles NE of High Wycombe on the A404

Nestling in the south-eastern corner of the Chiltern Hills, Amersham comprises a number of different settlements – including

The Old Town, Amersham

Amersham Old Town, Amersham-on-the-Hill and, effectively, Little Chalfont and CHESHAM BOIS – which have blossomed into a dormitory conurbation for London commuters. The rash of recent buildings built since the creation of 'Metroland', when the Metropolitan line stormed Buckinghamshire's rural barricades in 1889, includes some structures of mind-bogglingly mock antiquity. But enough remains of the genuinely old to make Amersham worth a visit.

Amersham Old Town exudes an air of unpretentious affluence, with its wide main street exhibiting a display of mellow 16th- and 17th-century houses. Broadway, as it is suitably called, is highlighted by the prominent 17th-century Market Hall whose single upper storey (now used for arts and craft exhibitions) is supported by brick arches surrounding the market floor at ground level. To the west, where Broadway becomes Amersham High St, a variety of old cottages and coaching inns recall the town's history as a staging post on the road from London to AYLESBURY and Oxford. Like many of the buildings on High St, The King's Arms, on the south side of High St not far from the Market Hall, dates from the 16th century, and still displays the arms of King Henry VIII.

Nearby, at the junction of the northern side of High St with Mill St, is the late 17th-century Mill House, under which flows the River Misbourne – in reality, little more than a brook. Alongside the Misbourne, a public footpath runs at the foot of the High St's cottage gardens, emerging into Barn Meadow, a public recreation ground for the townsfolk of Amersham.

🏛 **Amersham Museum**, at 49 High St, houses a display of historical artefacts from locally-found fossils, through Roman remains, to dairying bygones and other reminders of the area's agricultural and industrial heritage.

⛪ **St Mary's Church**, accessible via Church St, just to the east of the Market Hall, is attractively set in a churchyard with a variety of mature trees and views to the wooded Chilterns beyond. The large, square-towered, flint-stone edifice dates from the 12th century. The North Chapel was added 300 years later in 1480, and the whole church extensively restored in 1870.

Inside the church, six newly recast bells were dedicated in 1983 – a further six were added in 1993 – and a scene of the Nativity was painted above the altar in 1988 by local artist David Morris. There are some splendid tombs, notably of members of the Drake family, local squires and benefactors, who were laid to rest between the 17th and the 19th centuries. The Drakes also figure in some of the church's many fine brasses.

On the interior wall immediately above the main entrance is displayed a large royal coat of arms, in loyal adherence to the instructions of King Henry VIII, whose Act of Supremacy of 1535 ordained that the royal arms be displayed in every church. The original arms were mislaid during the 1870 restoration, and those now on display were installed in 1975, made from a cast of the arms used at the coronation of Queen Elizabeth II.

🏛 The elegant white mansion of **Shardloes** (picture, p. 41) sits at the far western end of the Old Town, where High St rejoins the A413 by-pass. Built by Stiff Leadbetter in 1758 and set in rolling parkland overlooking a lake drawn from the Misbourne, it is now converted into flats. Formerly, however, it was the home of the Drake family, who among other benefactions built a delightful array of almshouses in 1657.

The newer, northern, part of town, **Amersham-on-the-Hill** (known locally as 'top Amersham'), has much less character than its older neighbour, and owes its existence to the railway station now shared between British Rail and London Underground. However, it does contain the town's main shopping centre, leisure facilities, police and fire stations, law courts, and the offices and administrative headquarters of Chiltern District Council. The Martyrs' Memorial off Station Road (from where it is signposted) was erected in 1931 by the

Protestant Alliance to commemorate the burning at the stake at that spot of a number of Protestants in the early 16th century.

To the east, **Little Chalfont**, with a London Underground station of its own (Chalfton & Latimer) is primarily a commuter village, to all intents and purposes absorbed by Amersham. Before the arrival of the Metropolitan Railway it was scarcely more than a collection of local farms, some of which dated back to the Domesday Book. Since then, it has developed into one of Metroland's most successful outposts.

Amersham Museum: Easter–Oct, Sat, Sun and BH pm. Tel: 0494 725754.

ASHENDON

Map p.148, F4
2½ miles S of A41 near Waddesdon.

Situated nearly 500 ft above sea level, the tiny village of Ashendon commands an impressive view across the western part of the Vale of Aylesbury to nearby Waddesdon Manor. Including the adjoining hamlets of **Upper** and **Lower Pollicott**, the settlement consists of a few houses, a church and a pub, the Red Lion.

⛪ St Mary's Church contains the defaced effigy of a 13th-century cross-legged knight in the chancel. Made of Purbeck marble, its origins are uncertain. Some histories claim that the knight was a crusader, some that he was a member of the Cressy or Stafford families, while others say that the figure is the effigy of a Sir John Bucktot. The church architecture is mixed: the building has a Norman nave, a 17th-century pulpit and a 19th-century chancel.

ASTON ABBOTS

Map p.150, D2
3 miles SW of Wing off the A418

A modest village in Aylesbury Vale, Aston Abbotts has a scattering of 16th- and 17th-

century houses, a church and several pubs, one of which, the Royal Oak, has an interesting collection of Victorian and older domestic gadgetry.

The **Abbey** that gives the village its name is in fact an 18th-century country house on the site of a retreat used by the medieval abbots of St Albans. The house, a private home, is off Moat Lane to the south-west of the village; traces of the moat that surrounded the original building can still be seen.

A previous occupant of the present house was Rear Admiral Sir James Clark Ross, who discovered the position of the North magnetic Pole in 1831 and subsequently commanded an unsuccessful Antarctic expedition in 1839.

More recently, the Abbey was the home of Czech President Eduard Benes and his government in exile during World War II; his foreign minister Jan Masaryk lived a mile and a half away, on the other side of the A418 at WINGRAVE. It was at the Abbey that they planned the assassination of the Nazi Gestapo chief Reinhard Heydrich. The only visible sign of the Czech presence is a commemorative lime tree planted on the approach to the house and a bus shelter (on the A418 at the Aston Abbotts turn-off) that Benes gave to the villagers to protect them from the elements.

⛪ St James's Church, just north of the village green, contains two East windows in memory of Admiral Ross, who is buried in the churchyard. St James's has a 15th-century tower with a stair projection and was largely rebuilt in the 19th century by the prolific church restorer George Edmund Street. A plaque inside dated 1960 was presented by a citizen of Hartford, Connecticut, USA, whose ancestors left Aston Abbotts bound for Salem, Massachusetts in 1630, and evidently thrived there.

At Lines Hill, along the road south-west out of the village to WEEDON, faint outlines in the meadow to the left are all that remain of the former village of Burston. The victim of plague according to some accounts, the village was more probably wiped out by enclosures of common land in Elizabethan times.

35

ASTON CLINTON

Map p.150, F3
3 miles E of Aylesbury on the A41

Strung out along the busy A41 that brutally divides it, Aston Clinton begs for and may yet receive a by-pass to relieve it from the steady stream of London–Aylesbury traffic passing through it night and day.

Like other villages in the area, it bears the stamp of the Rothschild family, in this case Sir Anthony de Rothschild, who bought Aston Clinton Park in 1851. The house was demolished in 1960 (the park is now used by Buckinghamshire County Council) but the Rothschild influence lives on in the form of the Anthony Hall, built in 1884 and later given to the village, and two of the village schools, one of which was built to indulge his daughter's passion for teaching.

Another village teacher was the writer Evelyn Waugh, who taught at a prep school here between 1925 and 1927 and wrote much of his novel *Decline and Fall* at the same time. His memoirs make copious references to the 18th-century **Bell Inn** on the main road, still a highly-rated hostelry.

However, Waugh never experienced any of Aston Clinton's freak whirlwinds, which three times since World War II (latterly in 1984) have howled through the village, ripping up roofs and causing havoc.

⛪ St Michael and All Angels' Church, on the edge of the old Rothschild park, is a 13th- and 14th-century building of flint and stone, with a fairly new tower. Among the great of Aston buried there is Viscount Lake, who captured Delhi for the British Empire.

ASTWOOD

Map p.155, B1
6 miles NE of Newport Pagnell on the A422

The tiny settlement of Astwood, in the far north-east of the county by the Bedfordshire border, comprises little more than a church, an inn and a handful of houses; yet the Church of St Peter, on the main A422 road, suffered bomb damage during World War II. Bad luck was nothing new to the village: Astwoodbury House, described by the 18th-century county historian and one-time MP for Buckingham, Dr Browne Willis (see FENNY STRATFORD), as one of the finest in the county, was nevertheless demolished in 1799. All that remains is the former dovecote, once capable of housing some 300 nests and now converted into a private residence under the appropriate name of Dove House. Apparently only the local squire was permitted to have a dovecote, and his tenant farmers resented the birds growing fat from their cornfields.

AYLESBURY

Map p.149, F4
15 miles S of Milton Keynes on the A41

Until World War II, Aylesbury was a small market town, its narrow streets bunched around a market place and a church. The county town of Buckinghamshire since the reign of Henry VIII, it had escaped major development even when the Grand Union Canal reached the town in 1814, followed by the Great Western Railway in 1839 and the Metropolitan Railway half a century later. In the 1950s, though, like many towns around London, it began to receive the capital's overspill population. The rambling meadows and ponds where its famous ducks were bred gave way to new development, complete with a major ring road system, concrete neo-brutalist architecture and an accretion of large housing estates. The town was utterly transformed.

The 11-storey concrete County Hall, built in 1966 by Fred Pooley, became the symbol of the new Aylesbury. 'Pooley's Folly', as locals call it, is also a landmark for miles around the Vale. In 1970 it was followed by Friars Square Shopping

Disraeli's Library, Hughenden Manor, near Bradenham

Centre, its design so modern that Stanley Kubrick used it as a location for *A Clockwork Orange*, his film of Anthony Burgess's futuristic tale of urban violence and degradation. Its exposed concrete surfaces aged quickly and it had to close in 1990 for three years of radical remodelling. Now it is an airy, covered expanse where department stores and boutiques are scattered around iron fountains and fake marble columns.

The ancient heart of Aylesbury, now a tiny area compared with the town as a whole, still beats in the network of streets around St Mary's Church in the centre and in the isolated L-shape formed by Walton Terrace and Wendover Road at the southern end of the Walton St gyratory road.

St Mary's Church, just north of Market Square, stands on the highest ground in the town. Extensively restored by Sir George Gilbert Scott (see GAWCOTT) between 1850 and 1870, it has a 13th-century central tower topped by a 17th lead spire and is encased in 15th century battlements. Inside, behind the organ, there is a monument to Lady Lee (d. 1584), the widow of Sir Henry Lee who owned a manor house at QUARRENDON, and the damaged figure of a 14th-century knight. The windows hold a wealth of Victorian glass and there is a 12th-century font with a scalloped base.

The church is surrounded by a the 17th- and 18th-century St Mary's Square. **Prebendal House**, directly west of the church and hidden behind an elaborate gate, was the home of John Wilkes, MP for Aylesbury from 1757, a radical reformer and champion of press freedom. It is now used as offices. Next to it is **St Osyth's House**, a 17th-century former farm house which takes its name from the 7th-century Christian martyr born at QUARRENDON. Church St, leading south from St Mary's Square, contains 17th- and 18th-century almshouses (now old peoples' homes); the **Buckinghamshire County Museum**, formerly the Grammar School, is on the northern corner of the square. At the bottom of Church St is Temple Square.

With Church St, Temple St and Rickfords Hill, it forms a quiet sanctuary from the intrusive 20th century, where elegant old town houses still stand behind raised, railed pavements.

The County Museum is undergoing major refurbishment, and until 1995 only two galleries are open. When work is complete, it should be one of the most exciting museums in the region, with, among other delights, a special Children's Gallery to celebrate the works of author Roald Dahl, who lived in GREAT MISSENDEN.

Market Square, where markets are held on Wednesdays, Fridays and Saturdays, is in the town centre. The Clock Tower in the middle of the square was built in 1876, and on its south side stands the old County Hall, built by Thomas Harris in 1740.

Public executions were carried out from the building's main balcony until 1845. Inside, there is a wood-panelled courtroom on the first floor, still used as a Crown Court. Almost totally destroyed by an arsonist in 1970, it was faithfully restored down to the last detail – a recess behind the judge's seat to accommodate a chamber pot.

The **King's Head Hotel**, a National Trust property since 1928, is hidden in an alley at the north end of the Square. It has a large front window of 15th-century glass showing the royal arms of Henry VI and his bride, Margaret of Anjou. Cromwell stayed here after the Battle of Worcester in 1651, when Aylesbury was a Parliamentarian stronghold. The hotel bar is a vaulted, 15th-century hall, and still contains the chair on which Cromwell reputedly sat. The hotel is currently closed, but is expected to re-open by 1995 at latest.

Walton Terrace, a row of 17th- and 18th-century houses, is at the north end of Walton St, half a mile south of the town centre. With the part of adjacent Walton Road, it is the only other remnant of old Aylesbury.

County Museum: Mon–Sat, 10am–1.30pm and 2pm–5pm. Extended opening from 1995. Tel: 0296 696012.

Aylesbury Tourist Information Office: 0296 382308.

BEACHAMPTON

Map p.153, E2
5 miles NE of Buckingham on minor roads off the A422

Beachampton lies just south-east of the Great Ouse, which in former times powered two local mills. Small as it is, the village is the only significant settlement in a big sector of farmland to the west of Milton Keynes. The Domesday Book recorded 30 heads of household in the village. Today the population is only slightly larger, despite the growth of the nearby new city.

The manor was given to a Norman commander after the battle of Hastings. It is said that Henry VIII's sixth wife, Catherine Parr, lived at the the manor house and that Queen Anne inspected troops in the village. Only small parts of the old manor house remain, incorporated into the buildings at Hall Farm behind the gated wall in the field opposite the church.

St Mary's Church dates from the early 14th century but the striking tower is Victorian. Inside the church are some fine stone carvings, including a 17th-century statue of Sir Simon Bennett, Lord of the Manor at Calverton, two miles north-west.

Calverton is a quiet little hamlet today, but in the 17th century it had fine scandal. Sir Simon's wealthy widow, Grace, was murdered in the former manor house by a cousin, who was arrested, tried, and hanged from a gibbet in the village.

Two miles south-west of Beachampton, the hamlet of **Thornton** is a small group of brick and stone houses set in woodland close to the Great Ouse. There is a weir at this point on the river.

BEACONSFIELD

Map p.142, E2
5 miles SE of High Wycombe off M40 (J3)

Beaconsfield was once a bandit's paradise: a prosperous town on the main London-to-Oxford road, surrounded by dense woodland, it offered at the same time rich pickings and accessible hideaways. The woods have now receded, the road has slipped south to become the M40, and the bandits have gone. But the town still has an air of wealth.

There are not one but two Beaconsfields. **New Beaconsfield**, centred on the railway station to the north is a sprawl of dormitory housing which John Betjeman described in 1948 as 'a large umbrageous sample in the Metroland style.' Admirers of suburban architecture will appreciate it for its buildings alone. Others, however, will be more readily drawn by Bekonscot Model Village (see p.27; picture, p.31), some 4,500 square yards of miniature houses and railway track.

Old Beaconsfield, to the south, is a more enticing proposition. Predominantly 18th-century, it centres on a wide street of red-brick, creeper-clad shops and houses. There are a number of fine old coaching inns, one of which, the George, contains a staircase with sword-cuts made by highwayman Claude Duval while fighting off the Bow Street Runners. The Old Rectory and Capel House, two venerable half-timbered houses by the church, are Beaconsfield's oldest buildings. Capel House, which used to contain the curate, was converted and sold in 1978, and now bears the unfortunate name 'Olde Timbers'.

Beaconsfield has long attracted the wealthy, as is evidenced by the number of exquisitely proportioned Georgian houses. More surprisingly, however, it has also attracted those from the other end of the income scale: writers. Edmund Waller, a Civil War poet who saved his bacon by lauding Royalist and Roundhead alike, lived here, as did the 18th-century essayist and statesman Edmund Burke and his poet friend George Crabbe. Benjamin Disraeli, novelist and Prime Minister, was granted the title Earl of Beaconsfield by Queen Victoria. The American poet Robert Frost took rooms here. And G.K.Chesterton settled in a house midway between Old and New Beaconsfield – never having mastered the knack of shaving, and unwilling to appear partisan, he visited barbers in both towns on alternate mornings.

The **Church of St Mary and All Saints** stands in the centre of Old Beaconsfield. Its origins lie in the 13th century, but by 1869 the old structure had fallen into disrepair – due largely to the neglect of the previous vicar, who lived in Newgate Debtors Prison, and emerged only to conduct week-end services – and a massive rebuilding project was undertaken. The result is a large, welcoming, but unexceptional Victorian church. The interior contains memorials and wall plaques, including those to the Waller and Burke families, some ancient carved wood, and an extravagant Baroque armchair presented by Disraeli. Outside in the churchyard, a plinthed obelisk commemorates the poet Edmund Waller.

BIERTON

Map p.149, E4
2 miles NE of Aylesbury on the A418

Now almost a suburb of Aylesbury, Bierton is one of the many villages that continue to grow in a linear pattern along Aylesbury's arterial roads – in this case the busy A418. It is a mixture of old cottages and modern-day development; the most interesting building is the 400-year-old Red Lion pub on the Aylesbury Road.

Gib Lane, on the boundary between Bierton and the village of HULCOTT to the north-east, was the site of the last gibbet in the county. Its final customer, a murderous ratcatcher hanged in 1773, was said to have been on public show for 20 years before villagers kicked his remains into a ditch.

The small, largely 14th-century **St James's Church** has a surprisingly spacious interior. As well as a Norman font and unusual clerestory aisle windows, it contains a charming 17th-century monument to one Samuel Bosse, his wife

and 13 children, seven of them shown in cots behind their parents.

BLEDLOW

Map p.145, D2   ★★
2 miles SW of Princes Risborough off the B4009

Bledlow's half-timbered, brick and flint cottages are spread out along a tree-lined street, with some larger houses hidden in their gardens behind tall yew hedges. There is a small triangular green at one end, overlooked by a red brick farmhouse and low, white painted pub, The Lions of Bledlow, with open fields beyond. At the east end of the village is a large brick house designed as a workhouse school for girls. The Ridgeway long-distance footpath, on its route from Ivinghoe Beacon on the edge of the Chiltern Hills to Avebury in Wiltshire, passes just south of Bledlow, following the line of the Upper Icknield Way; the village is a popular stopping place for walkers.

Holy Trinity Church★★ sits in a large churchyard surrounded by horse chestnut trees. It is built of rough flint with stone quoining, has a low 12th-century nave with side aisles tucked beneath clerestory windows, a 13th-century tower and early 14th-century porch. The chancel was enlarged in the 14th century, as were the windows at that end of the nave. The shallow, beamed roof probably replaces a much steeper pitch, the outline of which can be seen on the face of the tower. The two side aisles are separated from the nave by sturdy columns with leaf carvings on the capitals and simple, pointed arches. On the walls can be seen the faint, sepia outline of 13th- or 14th-century wall paintings, including St Christopher on the north wall, with Adam and Eve depicted over the south door. There is a Norman, cup-shaped font with a scalloped base and fluted bowl.

The early 18th-century **Manor House**, across the lane from the church, has a

Shardloes, near Amersham

symmetrical front in pale brick, with rambling outbuildings and barns clustered at the rear, all set in formal gardens. The churchyard overlooks the Lyde, a deep ravine with lush, overgrown ponds, criss-crossed by landscaped paths and boarded walks. It belongs to the Manor House, but may be visited.

Lyde End, on the opposite side of the ravine from the church, is a group of houses designed in 1977. The award-winning design, by architects Aldington & Craig, is a good example of how modern houses can be sensitively inserted into an old village without resorting to a pastiche of existing styles.

The path beside the Lyde continues towards Pitch Green, on the Lower Icknield Way, where there is a 16th-century timber-framed mill. The tiny hamlet of **Horsenden**, a mile to the east, consists of a small church, a thatched cottage and Manor Farm. Another path climbs the hill behind Bledlow to the Ridgeway, from where it continues west to **Bledlow Cross**, a chalk cross of uncertain origin cut out of the hillside at Wain Hill on the Oxfordshire border.

BLETCHLEY

Map p.154, F2
3 miles S of Central Milton Keynes on the B4034

Despite being the largest of the three towns incorporated into the new city of MILTON KEYNES, Bletchley is now of little importance in its own right. Like STONY STRATFORD and WOLVERTON it is now effectively a suburb.

Although there has been a settlement at Bletchley for hundreds of years, as evidenced by the 12th-century church of St Mary (to the west of the centre, north of Church Green Road), it was not until Victorian times, and the arrival of the railway, that the town grew to a reasonable size. The main London-to-Scotland (West Coast) line bisects the town immediately to the west of the centre, and to the north of

Bletchley station is a sizeable goods depot and marshalling yard.

The most significant time in the history of Bletchley was during World War II, when the estate of Bletchley Park, to the north-west of the town centre off Church Green Road, was home to the vitally important and highly secret Government Code and Cypher School. At the height of its activities, Bletchley Park employed over 12,000 people; but because of the 30-year rule for the release of government documents, it has only been in relatively recent times that the full story has emerged. Some of the best academics and mathematicians of the day were recruited to break the highly-effective German codes, generated by their ingenious Enigma machines.

Astonishingly, in view of the number of people involved, the Germans apparently never knew of the work of Bletchley Park, nor even of its existence. Churchill once described the work there as his 'ultra secret', and credited it with shortening the war by three years; the code-breaking certainly saved very many lives, and the operation led directly to the development of the world's first computers.

Even after the war, the intelligence services continued to use Bletchley Park as a monitoring station, and not until 1987 was the 55-acre estate leased for commercial use by British Telecom and the Civil Aviation Authority. However, neither BT nor the CAA remained for long, and the entire estate was vacant by 1993.

Local residents have formed the Bletchley Park Trust to try to save the Park from dereliction and to establish a national museum dedicated to the intelligence services, the history of the computer – and, in view of the Park's recent use by the CAA, radar and air traffic control.

BOARSTALL TOWER

Map p.148, F2
2 miles N of Oakley off the B4011

Boarstall Tower was a strategic stronghold on the road to Oxford during the Civil War, changing hands many times during the course of the fighting. Originally the 14th-century moated mansion house of Sir John Handlo, all that is left now is the fortified gate house, its massive timber gates and behind these a moat and garden. The gatehouse is now owned by the National Trust and may be viewed by appointment.

♁ St James's Church is situated behind the garden wall linked to Boarstall Tower. The present church was built in 1818, although its contents are much older. There are monuments to a great landowning family, the Aubreys and Aubrey-Fletchers, as well as a Jacobean pulpit and a communion table dated 1615.

The **Boarstall Duck Decoy**, situated behind Manor Farm, a little to the north on the road to Brill, is a remnant of the ancient trade of wildfowling and one of only half a dozen left in England. Like Boarstall Tower, it is owned by the National Trust.

The decoy consists of an elaborate series of nets around the lake so arranged that they funnel into a narrow pipe. Highly trained dogs (the Dutch Kooikerhondje breed is used) drive ducks down the funnel into the pipe, from which they cannot escape.

Originally, the trapped birds would have found their way on to the dinner table but now they are ringed for study and released. Visitors can watch the procedure from a thatched hide: demonstrations are regularly performed.
Tower and Decoy: National Trust.
Tel: 0494 528051.

BOW BRICKHILL

Map p.154, E3
2 miles SW of Woburn Sands off the A5130

The Bow Brickhill Road out of WOBURN SANDS becomes the Woburn Sands Road once it enters the outskirts of Bow Brickhill village, and changes its name again in the centre of the village, at the junction with Church Road (to the left), to become Station Road. Church Road is steep and

narrow, leading not only to the village church of All Saints, some way up the hill on the right, but also deeper into the mixed woods of pine, beech, oak, sweet chestnut and ash on the fringes of the Duke of Bedford's estate. The wooded hill is the highest in the area, and it dominates the village of Bow Brickhill.

In the past the estate and the woods provided employment for the menfolk of Bow Brickhill, who felled and cut trees for railway sleepers and quarried ironstone from the sandy ridge. While much of the woodland remains commercial – providing, among other things, fencing posts, tool handles, hurling sticks, construction timber and pulp for the paper and board industry – significant areas of the wood, on both sides of Church Road, have been cleared to accommodate a championship golf course (Woburn), which has been the venue for some important events including the Dunhill Masters.

Bow Brickhill is the starting point for one of a number of country walks promoted by Milton Keynes Borough Council. Indeed there are three alternative walks from Bow Brickhill: six miles, three miles or a mile and a half, depending on your fitness and inclination. Depending on the time of year and the weather, walkers can be treated to a luxuriant carpet of bluebells, mixed with the delicate, spring green of the new foliage, or to a blaze of autumn yellows, reds and golds, interspersed with the evergreens of the pine trees – all enhanced by birdsong, squirrels and dappled sunlight. The Bow Brickhill walks are in leaflet number three in the series Countryside Walks published by Milton Keynes Borough Council, obtainable from various local public libraries.

♁ All Saints Church, in a dominant position 500 ft up on the hillside, is not easily accessible to its parishioners, whether by vehicle or on foot. By road, the church is a third of a mile or more up the steep hill of Church Road. There is a small clearing in the woods for parking, and then a walk of about 200 yds along a muddy track. By foot, it is a steep climb, partly along

Church Road, and then up a very rugged footpath. At the worst times of the year, it is hard to imagine the faithful of All Saints going to church in their Sunday-best shoes...and how the Victorian and Edwardian ladies managed, in their elegant, flowing, ankle-length dresses, is a mystery.

The church itself is small, square-towered, and possibly Norman in origin. Once a year, on a Saturday in September, the tower is open to the public. The vertigo-free may climb a narrow, steeply-winding, stone staircase, and then two steep, rickety and woodworm-ridden ladders. When they emerge at the top, they will be rewarded with a splendid view northwards to Milton Keynes.

The parishioners of All Saints are especially proud of the Bow Brickhill Hymn, written by village resident Dr Sidney Nicholson, who founded the Royal School of Music in 1927. Dr Nicholson was also organ master at Westminster Abbey, and annually brought the boys of the Westminster Choir to sing at All Saints.

BRADENHAM

Map p.146, E1 ★
3 miles NW of High Wycombe off the A4010

Few villages genuinely deserve to be described as unspoilt, but Bradenham, in the ownership of the National Trust since 1956, merits the title. Its flint and brick cottages line one side of a spacious, triangular green with a cricket pitch at its centre. At the top of the village the church and Manor House sit side by side. They overlook the green which slopes towards a broad vista of the wooded valley and the Vale of Aylesbury in the distance. At the bottom, beside the Wycombe road, is the Red Lion pub and the 18th-century Rectory.

⌂ The **White House**, also 18th-century, stands beside the green. It is a stuccoed, double-fronted, twin-gabled house in the Gothic style with weatherboarded outbuildings. The flint and red brick Nonconformist chapel, by a small pond, is now a Youth Hostel.

⌂ **St Botolph's Church**, of rough flint with stone quoining, has a squat tower and large, rendered side chapel. Its external appearance owes much to extensive restoration by G.E.Street in 1863 which included rebuilding the chancel and part of the nave. The simple interior has an open timber roof. The north chapel contains a monument to one Charles West (d.1684) and its east window includes an early example of 18th-century enamelled glass. The church has a lich-gate, erected in 1920 to commemorate those in the parish who died in the First World War.

⌂ **Bradenham Manor**, its large gardens separated from the churchyard by a high brick wall, is approached from the village green through wrought iron gates. It has an impressive 17th-century front of decorated brick, tall sash windows, steep roofs with small dormer windows and a row of slender brick chimneys. It was the last home of Isaac d'Israeli, who died in 1848 and is buried in the church. It was his son the 19th-century Prime Minister, Benjamin Disraeli, who in the same year acquired the nearby Hughenden Manor (see p.19). The house is now a business centre and not open to the public. A track skirts the Manor on the south side, climbing the wooded hillside to join a path that connects with Hughenden.

BRILL

Map p.148, F3
1½ miles NE of Oakley off the B4011

More than 600 ft above sea level, with excellent views in all directions, Brill is largely surrounded by its somewhat uneven common, which bears the scars of 600 years of clay-working to provide bricks, tiles and pots.

One of the many Elizabethan and Georgian houses in the village, the Sun

Brill Windmill

45

Hotel, in the High St, is said to be on site of the royal stables of Henry VIII.

Tram Hill, at the north end of the village, was until the 1930s, the terminus of the long-vanished Brill Tramway, built in 1872 by the Duke of Buckingham to connect his estate at Wotton Underwood with the main line seven miles away at Quainton Road.

Overlooking the village green is the 1841 Methodist Church and the 16th-century brick and tile Brill Manor House.

༈ **Brill Windmill** (picture, p.44) on the common is a good place to enjoy fine panoramic views over Oxfordshire and the Vale of Aylesbury. A post mill built in 1668, it is the last survivor of three mills once working in the village, at least one of which dated back to 1286. It is constructed of black weather-boarding with white sails, supported on wooden stilts now covered by a brick base.

⛪ **All Saints' Church**, standing behind yew trees in the High St on the village green, retains fragments of its 12th-century origins, a 15th-century tower and a 17th-century roof.

BUCKINGHAM

Map p.152, F4
10 miles SW of Milton Keynes on the A421

Buckingham straddles the Great Ouse on the north-west edge of the county. The oldest part of the town stands on high ground tucked into a deep bend of the river, and there is a good view over the whole area from the highest point. But the narrow streets are usually packed with vehicles and it is wise to seek somewhere to park lower down. Parking behind the community centre off the High St is a conveniently short walk through a new shopping arcade back to the main road.

The High St is dominated by the **Old Gaol (picture, p.49)**, a mock castle built in 1758 by Lord Cobham of nearby Stowe (see p.21) and used for the Summer Assizes. These important court sessions

were moved to Aylesbury 90 years later and the Old Gaol has been converted for community use. Buckingham's position as county town, conferred by Alfred the Great, had already long gone the same way as its assizes. Henry VIII transferred the status to Aylesbury which is both closer to London and more centrally located in this long county. Today, even the district council is run from Aylesbury, and uphill from the Old Gaol stands another casualty of shifting power: the redundant town hall, a large brick building now used by businesses.

Half way between the Old Gaol and the former town hall is the old bull ring. Once, cattle were traded here (though sheep were a more common sight, since Buckingham was an important centre for the wool trade). Now it is crammed with the usual stalls on Saturday market day, while for the rest of the week it is a car park.

A few yards north-west of the bull ring is Buckingham's oldest building, the **Chantry Chapel**, which has a Norman doorway dated 1260. After the Reformation the place was used as a school until outgrown and is now a National Trust property. After the Chapel, a right turn leads to West St and Castle House. Charles I and Catherine of Aragon were among the notables who stayed in this building; its early 18th-century façade of red brick and stone dressing masks the original structure. It is now used for offices.

A turn to the south into School Lane leads to St Rumbold's Lane, named after a 7th-century baby who died aged three days: not uncommon in days of high infant mortality. Rumbold, though, earned his canonization by asking aloud for baptism. Wells in the town were named after him, and the story attracted a trickle of pilgrims for centuries.

At the end of St Rumbold's Lane, on the right in Church St is the former congregational church, now used by the University of Buckingham. This institution opened in 1976 as Britain's first independent university and has since occupied and refurbished a number of important buildings in the town. Perhaps the most notable is the early Tudor **Manor House**, complete with authentic twisted chimney stack, further down Church St. Elizabeth I once dined in great style at this house. To the left at the end of St Rumbold's Lane is the entrance to the grounds of the Church of St Peter and St Paul. This large church was built between 1777 and 1781 but considerably altered 80 years later by the architect Sir George Gilbert Scott, who was born in the local village of GAWCOTT. The church stands on Castle Hill, the name being the sole remaining indication that there were once fortifications here. The hill gives a fine view of Buckingham's predominantly Georgian core, now surrounded by new housing.

A large number of the many 18th-century buildings were put up because a fire in 1725 destroyed a third of the town's 400 homes. The northern exit from the churchyard is towards Castle St where the fire started at the Swan and Castle coaching inn. Ironically at least part of the inn survived and it is possible to see the room where Oliver Cromwell was said to have held a meeting, although the town was a Royalist stronghold.

Castle St emerges at the side of the town hall where a right turn down Bridge St might provide some light relief. Here can be found a shop selling theatrical costumes, fancy dress and period clothes with a particularly good stock of 1960s originals.

There is also a pub in Bridge St, the **New Inn**, with a large cellar room restricted to family use and protected by a sign warning 'no unaccompanied adults'. Books, games and comfortable seats make it a civilized alternative for families often exiled to the chill of garden benches.

BUCKLAND

Map p.150, F3
½ mile N of Aston Clinton off the A41

A small, leafy village at the foot of the Chilterns, Buckland effectively merges into adjacent **Aston Clinton**. It is a mixture of farmhouses, notably the timber-framed Church Farm, and more modern bungalows.

All Saints' Church, in the centre of the village, is a grey flint building with a whitewashed interior. Mainly Victorian (the tower was rebuilt in 1894) it has a 13th-century font inside with a scalloped base.

At the end of Buckland Road, where it joins the A41, the now disused Wendover Arm of the Grand Union Canal branches under the road toward the nearby Hertfordshire border.

BURNHAM

Map p.142, C2
3 miles NW of Slough off the A435

Burnham is more a suburb of sprawling Slough than a true village. Yet thanks to the designation of its High St as a conservation area, it has retained something of its original identity.

The early 13th-century **St Peter's Church** is in Church St, at the southern end of the High St. There are some fine brasses and monuments, and on a pillar a curious medieval graffito: its inscriber reckoned the pope of the day was a 'knave' and a 'vilin'.

The ruins of Burnham Abbey, founded in 1266 and dissolved in the Reformation, are just south of the village off Lake End Road, close to the M4. From there, it is a short walk east to the private **Huntercombe Manor** in Huntercombe Lane South. From the outside, it has a late 19th-century appearance, but the reportedly beautiful interior dates in parts from the 14th century.

Perhaps the most interesting building in the vicinity is **Dorneywood**, a 1920s country house a mile or so north-east of the village. It is the perquisite of the Chancellor of the Exchequer, much as

Chequers (see ELLESBOROUGH) is at the disposal of the Prime Minister. The house itself is strictly off-limits to the public, but the gardens are accessible.

Burnham finds its greatest glory in the **Burnham Beeches**, 500 acres of ancient woodland extending northwards from the edge of the village. Purchased by the Corporation of London in 1879, and dedicated for public use in perpetuity, they are a haven for wildlife as well as place of magical quality for strollers, who find themselves in a kind of arboreal cathedral. Many of the trees are extraordinarily ancient: the greatest, appropriately known as 'His Majesty', had a girth of 29ft 1in and was 600 years old when it succumbed to the hurricane of 1987. And the shapes they have grown into, after centuries of pollarding, are no less remarkable than they were 200 years ago, when the poet Thomas Gray wrote of Burnham's 'old, fantastic roots.'

CASTLETHORPE

Map p.153, C3
4 miles NW of Milton Keynes off the A508

Castlethorpe abuts the Northamptonshire border in the north-west of the county, and is bisected by the main London-to-Glasgow west coast railway line. The nearby railway town of WOLVERTON (now incorporated within the new city of MILTON KEYNES) provided employment for Castlethorpe's menfolk in the last century and the earlier part of this century, although farming, of course, is still an important activity locally.

The **Church of St Simon and St Jude** – prominent on high ground in the village centre – is one of the older churches of the area, dating originally from Norman times. The main body of the church, in the familiar, local, cream-coloured stone, has undergone some restoration in recent years. The square tower (yet to undergo similar restoration) is built of a mixture of the same cream-coloured stone and a

brown sandstone, giving the tower an interesting multi-coloured appearance, particularly attractive in sunlight.

To the west of the church, in an adjacent field, is a prominent mound – all that remains of the former Castlethorpe Castle, destroyed in 1215.

CHALFONT ST GILES

Map p.147, F2
3 miles S of Amersham off the A413

The two neighbouring settlements of Chalfont St Giles and CHALFONT ST PETER were recorded together in the Domesday Book as Chefunte (literally, 'Chalk Spring'). In 1237, however, they parted company, each taking its name from its own parish church. Of the two, Chalfont St Giles is the smaller but distinctly the more attractive.

The centre of this village is about 400 yds south-west of The Pheasant Inn crossroad on the A413. The inn itself dates from the 16th century, and Cromwell's troops camped in the meadows to the rear, overlooking Chalfont St Giles. The east window of St Giles's church was said to have been damaged by Cromwell's artillery and, as recently as 1861, roundhead cannon balls were found embedded in its masonry.

Approaching from the crossroad, Pheasant Hill becomes High St, with the village green on the left. Overlooked by The Merlin's Cave, a Tudor-style public house, the green bears an interesting sign, erected in 1953 to commemorate the coronation of Queen Elizabeth II but with a picture depicting St Giles forgiving the French king for shooting his pet deer. At one end of the green a sizeable hollow marks the site of the old village pond – now, alas, dried-up.

For a settlement that is sited so firmly in Metroland, Chalfont St Giles retains a pleasing variety of medieval architecture. There are a number of timbered 16th-century buildings, including John Milton's

The Old Gaol, Buckingham

Cottage (see p.28; picture, p.65) set on the High St some 300 yds uphill from the green.

🔔 The **Church of St Giles** is hidden away on the village green side of High St, with only its square tower visible above the roof-tops. The church is approached through a coaching gate leading from High St, and then through an unusual, double-swinging lich-gate (somewhat like a see-saw on its edge). The church is built of the familiar local flint, with stone and hard chalk dressing, and dates originally from Norman times. The chancel was rebuilt, though, in the 13th century, and the south aisle and the tower were added in the succeeding 200 years. In the 19th century it was restored by G.E. Street.

🏛 On the other side of the A413, **The Vache** is an Elizabethan mansion now converted to office accommodation. The house is on the site of a former Norman mansion, and takes its name from the de la Vache family who were granted the land by King William I. In the grounds is a monument to the 18th-century explorer Captain James Cook, whose friend and patron, Admiral Sir Hugh Palliser lived in the house, which Cook often visited. Sir Hugh was merely returning a compliment: Cook named a cape and a bay in New Zealand after his host, and an island after the house itself.

CHALFONT ST PETER

Map p.142, A4
1 mile N of Gerrards Cross on the A413

Larger than its Domesday-twin, CHALFONT ST GILES, and with less character, Chalfont St Peter merges almost imperceptibly with GERRARDS CROSS to the south. Chalfont St Peter has expanded considerably over the past half-century and is now a commuter village of some size with the M25 London orbital motorway less than a mile distant.

Most of the buildings on the High St are relatively new, inter-war architecture rubbing shoulders with the functional but uninspiring structures of modern times. However, a number of old buildings still recall the village's pre-industrial heritage, among them The George and The White Hart, two 16th-century coaching inns which retain most of their original timbers.

🍷 **The Greyhound** is also 16th-century – although there has been an inn here since 1407 – and incorporates a tunnel said to have been used as a bolt-hole by the infamous Judge Jefferies who presided at the Bloody Assizes in 1685.

🔔 Early references to the **Church of St Peter** suggest that it was built originally in 1133. In 1708, however, the steeple collapsed and destroyed much of the building. The church was subsequently rebuilt using red-brick with stone dressing, but much of its 18th-century character was swept away by further alterations in 1854 and 1965.

CHEARSLEY

Map p.145, A1   ★
2 miles NE of Long Crendon off the B4011

Once a thriving manufactory of pins and needles, Chearsley is set on a steep slope above the River Thame. At its heart lies Upper Green, lined with a mixture of brick or timber-framed cottages, farm buildings and more recent houses, and crossed by narrow lanes that radiate out from the village centre. The Old Farm House, a large, chequered brick house with a twin-gabled roof, is one of a number of 'homestalls' or homesteads. Its weatherboarded outbuildings are now converted to houses. The Bell pub is a small, white rendered and thatched building on the corner of the green. Church Lane winds down the hill from the pub, flanked by a row of ivy-clad, brick cottages and high walls, until it reaches the church at Lower Green. Lower Green Farmhouse, opposite the church, is 15th- or 16th-century.

At the bottom of the lane a footpath leads across water meadows to the willow-lined banks of the River Thame. From here it continues to CUDDINGTON, a mile east, or over the Dad Brook to HADDENHAM, a mile and a half to the south. Further up the hill, another path leads west to LONG CRENDON, passing Notley Abbey (see LONG CRENDON).

St Nicholas's Church, was originally a chapel of ease served by the monks from Notley Abbey, until claimed for ordinary parish use following the Dissolution. Built of local limestone, it has a staggered, 13th-century nave and chancel and a large, castellated tower. Its whitewashed interior features an exposed tie-beam roof, a shallow chancel arch which is offset from the nave, and a wooden gallery across the face of the tower. There is a Norman font and some simple box pews, copies of those at Haddenham. On the north wall are the painted Royal Arms of George II; those of George III hang on the west gallery. An evocative exhibit is a copy of the Manor Survey of 1763, which shows the ancient pattern of fields with their names, and in which the lanes are all referred to as 'ways'.

CHEDDINGTON

Map p.150, E4
2 miles NW of Ivinghoe off the B488

Largely consisting of post-war housing, Cheddington has a church – St Giles' – with traces of its Norman origins, a 14th-century chancel, a 15th-century tower and aisle and a carved Jacobean pulpit. The village is understandably somewhat coy about its more recent history, and no signposts guide visitors to the scene of Cheddington's most dramatic event: the Great Train Robbery of 1963, which catapulted it into the headlines of every national newspaper in the Western world.

The Glasgow–London night mail train was hijacked on the embankment at Bridego Bridge half a mile north of Cheddington station, then shunted a mile further to Sears Crossing, where the gang – one of whom, Ronnie Biggs, still thrives in exile in Rio de Janeiro – unloaded £2.6 million in used banknotes.

The five-mile embankment, built in the 1830s from chalk taken from nearby Pitstone quarry, still dominates the

landscape to the east of the village where it crosses the Grand Union Canal. South-west of the village there are signs of much older earthworks. The still-visible hillside lynchets – agricultural terraces cut as part of the Saxon open field system – are only now gradually becoming overgrown.

CHENIES

Map p.147, E3
3 miles E of Amersham, off the A404

The small village of Chenies (pronounced 'Chainies'), lies adjacent to the Hertfordshire border and only some two miles outside London's M25 orbital motorway. But a less metropolitan setting it is hard to imagine. The village has successfully maintained its peaceful, rustic ambience, to the extent that it is much in demand as a period setting for film and television dramas. Immediately west of the village green is a tree-lined drive which leads to Chenies Manor House (see p.14), ancient home of the Earls and Dukes of Bedford whose ancestors, the Cheney family, gave the village its name.

The Church of St Michael stand just outside the gates to the Manor House. Built of local flint, with stone dressings, it houses the Bedfords' mortuary chapel, said to be the most complete collection of family monuments in any English church. Every late Earl and Duke of Bedford is interred within the chapel, and the churchyard contains the remains of many of the Duchesses, sons and daughters of the Russell family, for centuries one of the most powerful of England's aristocratic clans.

The three-mile drive from Chenies to CHESHAM, along the road in the Chess valley, is very rewarding, with views over some of the most beautiful countryside in this part of the county. You will observe **Latimer House** (see LATIMER), prominent and impressive to the north; horses and cattle grazing the rich water meadows; and a wonderful variety of trees, clad in different hues at any time of the year but

absolutely ablaze with colour on a bright, autumn day.

CHESHAM

Map p.147, D1
2 miles N of Amersham on the A416

Now occupying an area of about six square miles in the valley of the River Chess, the present town of Chesham was established by the Saxons. However, Stone Age, Bronze Age and Roman relics all suggest that there has been a settlement here for far longer. The arrival of the railway in 1889, and the consequent ease of travel to and from London, led to the growth of the modern town we see today. Chesham is one of the two, final, north-westerly outposts of the Metropolitan Line – the other being nearby AMERSHAM.

Chesham High St was pedestrianized in 1990, but at a heavy price: the ring road constructed to take the former High St traffic now cuts painfully through some older parts of the town centre near to High St. Church St, with many of Chesham's oldest buildings, is now bisected by the new road and must be reckoned a major casualty.

Not all of Chesham's character has been lost. On the western side of High St, the George and Dragon is an ancient coaching inn whose interior bears wall paintings dating from 1715. In a shop next door to the George and Dragon, one Arthur Liberty carried on business as a haberdasher; in 1875, his son went on to establish the famous Liberty's store in London's Regent St.

Another old Cheshamite, Roger Crabbe achieved fame as the real-life Mad Hatter, to be immortalized by Lewis Carroll as the character in 'Alice in Wonderland'. Crabbe suffered severe head injuries during the Civil War, and was later sentenced to death by Cromwell for indiscipline. But he was pardoned and opened a hat shop in Chesham where in an effort to practise

Christianity as he understood it, he lived on little but bran and turnip-tops, dressed in sackcloth, and gave away his modest income to the poor. He even published an autobiography, explaining how his diet and costume allowed him to 'live with three Farthings a week.'

🏛 **St Mary's Church** is reached from Church St, via a cobbled path leading up a slight incline past the 18th-century Rectory. Its well-kept churchyard is a peaceful oasis after the rumble and grime of the traffic below, with good views of the surrounding Chiltern Hills. The large flint church, with its central square tower surmounted by a lead spire, dates back to the 12th century, and has been little affected by Victorian restoration.

In the churchyard is a mausoleum to the Lowndes family, of whom William Lowndes, Secretary to the Treasury under Queen Anne, built **The Bury** in 1716, an impressive manor house immediately adjacent to the churchyard and with its own entrance off Church St. The celebrated Committee of 'Ways and Means' of the House of Commons took its name from the Lowndes family motto. The Bury now provides suites of office accommodation.

♣ **Lowndes Park**, immediately to the north and west of the churchyard and The Bury, and abutting the inner ring road, comprises 28 acres of public recreational facilities, including lawns, play areas, flower-beds, a bandstand, and Skottowes Pond, with resident ducks and geese.

🏛 **Chesham Bois Manor**, on the southern outskirts towards Amersham, is a castle-like building of flint stone, simultaneously grotesque and intriguingly attractive. Now a residential home for the elderly, it was originally called Chesham House, but its then occupants somewhat pompously changed its name to Chesham Bois Manor when they bought the lordship of the manor of the nearby village of CHESHAM BOIS from the Duke of Bedford.

Chesham

CHESHAM BOIS

Map p.147, D1
1 mile S of Chesham off the A416

Although named after nearby CHESHAM, the village of Chesham Bois (pronounced 'boys') has effectively been swallowed by the northward expansion of AMERSHAM's commuter belt, with which it merges almost indistinguishably. Its name derives from one William du Bois who acquired the local manor house and family chapel in 1213, although there is evidence to suggest that the manor house was earlier granted by the Norman conqueror, King William I, to his kinsman, the Bishop of Bayeux.

The house passed through the ownership of the Cheyne family – of whom Sir Thomas Cheyne was imprisoned in the Tower of London in 1414 for heresy – and into the possession of the Russell family, later to become the Dukes of Bedford. It was demolished in 1812, but the chapel now forms the chancel of the present-day Church of St Leonard in Bois Lane, where the first Labour prime minister, Ramsay MacDonald, once owned a weekend cottage.

CHETWODE

Map p.148, A2
4 miles NW of Steeple Clayton on minor roads off the A421

Chetwode is a tiny, out-of-the-way parish in north Buckinghamshire, the site of an Augustinian Priory founded in 1245. No coherent village existed here until the 15th century, when the Priory's lack of sponsors and consequent grinding poverty forced its dissolution, long before the Reformation.

Indeed, it was not so much dissolved as recycled, for its substantial buildings provided stone for Chetwode's first inhabitants, while the Priory's surviving chancel became the village church. Today, the village consists of a scattering of large houses (some of them still working farmhouses) around the church. To the west is the old railway line, to the east is **Chetwode Manor**, a fine red-brick Jacobean mansion.

The village was named after the 12th-century landowner John Chetwode, who became a hero for successfully hunting down a ferocious wild boar that had roamed the area for years, killing children. He speared the beast after a bloody battle, and the story is still told in the village today, eight centuries later.

⛪ The Church of St Mary and St Nicholas has some of the first stained glass windows made in Buckinghamshire, probably in the 14th century. The tall, slim lancet windows are almost as tall as the church itself. More glass was added in 1842 in a skilfully matching style. There are also some interesting pews, including a family pew with its own built-in fireplace.

CHICHELEY

Map p.154, B4
3 miles NE of Newport Pagnell on the A422

Chicheley is nothing more than a hamlet, though it does have a pub – The Chester Arms – immediately fronting the northern side of the A442. It is dominated by Chicheley House and Chicheley Hall, both to the south side of the A422 down Hall Lane (opposite The Chester Arms). Chicheley House is an imposing white mansion, clearly visible from Hall Lane across a splendid private lawn.

⛪ Chicheley Hall* is grander still. It is at the far end of Hall Lane, past Chicheley House and the medieval, square-towered church of St Lawrence. The Hall was built in the early 18th century for Sir John Chester and was acquired by the Beatty family in 1952. Noted for its Georgian architecture, its internal wood panelling and its interesting garden features, Chicheley Hall now houses many artefacts and memorabilia of the First World War Admiral Beatty, including a collection of fine sea paintings.
Chicheley Hall: Sun, BH only, 2.30–5.00pm. Tel: 0234 391252.

CHILTON

Map p.144, A4
3 miles E of Oakley off the B4011

A small village with a superb setting on the southern slope of a limestone ridge, Chilton has a magnificent view for several miles across Aylesbury Vale. The village has a number of brick and timber-framed cottages, and the 18th-century stone and brick-pilastered Townhill Farm, but it is dominated by its great house.

Chilton House was originally the home of Sir John Croke, one of Thomas Cromwell's Clerks in Chancery, who acquired the parish at the Dissolution of the Monasteries. It was rebuilt in 1740 by Chief Justice Carter who modestly ordered his architects to copy the original plans for Buckingham House (which later became known as Buckingham Palace), although it still features the Tudor chimneys of its predecessor. The house is not open to the public but can be seen through its splendid wrought ironwork entrance.

St Mary's Church, in Church Road, is mainly 13th-century, with a 14th-century tower. It features the striking figure of a 13th-century knight placed high up on the outside wall of the tower. Inside are some fine monuments, including the tomb of Sir John Croke, (d. 1608) and the enormous tomb of Chief Justice Carter (d. 1755). On a very different scale, a simple wooden cross brought from the Flanders battlefield of Loos commemorates two local brothers killed during World War I.

THE CLAYDONS

Map p.149, B1
4 SW of Winslow by minor roads off the A413

There are four settlements around Claydon House (see p.14), all once part of the Verney estate. **Middle Claydon**, where the great house stands, consists only of a few buildings associated with the estate, and is scarcely a village at all.

Steeple Claydon, to the west, is the largest of the four, having expanded rapidly after World War II when production soared at the nearby brickworks at **Calvert**. (Ironically, the new brick-makers were at first housed in American aluminium pre-fabs.) Mainly brick-built, the village still has some thatched houses. Its **Church of St Michael** stands on a hill in the eastern end of the village, a 14th-century building with a spire added by Victorian restorers.

The village library was supported by Florence Nightingale who often stayed at Claydon House. Her cheque for £50 is on display.

East Claydon grew up around crossroads a mile to the east, which are still lined by its black-and-white cottages, now privately owned. They were formed by joining together two or more of the tiny cottages formerly occupied by estate workers. The finest building is the 17th-century **White House**, formerly an estate dower house. **St Mary's Church** is to the south-east. With a stone tower, the church was heavily restored by Sir George Gilbert Scott; there is a 13th-century chapel inside.

St Mary's also serves the estate hamlet of **Botolph Claydon** less than a mile to the south. The best dwelling here is the early 18th-century **Botolph House**, a fine brick building and another Verney dower house.

COLNBROOK

Map p.143, E1
3 miles SE of Slough off the A4

Colnbrook is the most southern point of Buckinghamshire. Now much boxed in by trunk roads, motorways and reservoirs, it is also afflicted by aircraft noise from Heathrow Airport, whose outer perimeter is a mile to the east. Formerly, the village was an important and occasionally dangerous staging post for travellers along the old London–Bath road.

In the 17th century, the **Ostrich Inn** in the High St was only one of many when its murderous landlord made it infamous. Thomas Jarman had a special treatment for selected guests – those travelling alone, and preferably not expected at a particular destination. In the middle of the night, their bed abruptly tilted over and slid them into a vat of boiling water. The profitable business continued for years until a bolting horse was recognized by a friend of its murdered owner; with 13 victims officially to their credit, Jarman and his wife were hanged.

Today drinkers at the High St pub, which dates from 1106 and claims to be England's third-oldest inn, receive a much friendlier welcome, and they can inspect a working model of Jarman's killing machine.

COOMBE HILL

Map p.146, B2
1½ miles SW of Wendover off the A413

Its dramatic escarpment topped by a huge monument to the Buckinghamshire men who died in the Boer War, Coombe Hill, at more than 850 ft above sea level, is the the highest point in the Chilterns. A wide, open space in the middle of woodlands, the hill and the grassy pasture behind it are now owned by the National Trust, a gift to the nation by Lord Lee of Fareham in 1912.

In summer, the hilltop is often thronged with picnickers and kite-fliers; many others are drawn there simply for the views, which on a clear day are spectacular. A plaque by the monument points out the Cotswolds (up to 55 miles away), Brill Hill (13 miles away) and the best available view of the inaccessible Chequers, the Prime Ministerial retreat and another gift from Lord Lee (see ELLESBOROUGH).

CUBLINGTON

Map p.150, C1
3 miles west of Wing off the A418

Had the government accepted the recommendations of the infamous Roskill

Report in the early 1970s, Cublington would by now be under the runways of the third London airport. Instead, this sleepy little village, where old and new houses nestle comfortably together, survives intact with only a commemorative spinney planted by Buckinghamshire County Council to remind residents of their victory over the planners.

Featured in the Domesday Book, Cublington apparently moved about half a mile at some point around 1400. The site of the old village, now classified as an ancient monument, can still be made out at the end of Ridings Way to the south-west. A footpath runs through it, and the scant remains of a Norman castle can still be seen: a small mound at a spot called The Beacon.

St Nicholas's Church, a 15th-century building, contains the oldest parish chest still in use in Buckinghamshire, dating from Norman times. The figures of a monkey and a man can be seen carved into corbels on the chancel arch. Victorian oil lamps still light the church, although now they have been converted to electricity.

CUDDINGTON

Map p.149, F1
5 miles W of Aylesbury off the A418

An appealing village with many thatched cottages built of witchert (see HADDENHAM), Cuddington centres on its green where roads span out towards the flat water meadows of the River Thame. It won Buckinghamshire's Best-Kept Village award in 1985 and it is obvious that its people still take immense pride in their gardens: it is regularly nominated for other competitions, notably 'Britain in Bloom'.

St Nicholas's Church has a tranquil, stone-walled graveyard surrounded by elms. Originally 12th-century it has been much restored over the centuries with a final renovation by the architect and

Cymbeline's Mount viewed from Coombe Hill

church builder G.E.Street in 1857. Inside is a 12th-century, tub-type font and some interesting carving.

Across the road from the church is the stone-built **Tyringham House**, the former manor house, which features the date 1609 over its doorway.

DENHAM

Map p.143, B1
2 miles NW of Uxbridge on the A40

Denham's charm has survived the building of the M40 motorway next door and sprawling London suburbia. Its tree-lined High St (formally called 'Village Road') is made up of individually designed, substantial houses, most with a distinctive character of their own. Views of it occasionally appear on television and cinema screens in films that may have made at the Rank studios in the village. There is a green at the end of the street.

⛪ **St Mary's Church**, set amid trees at the other end of the High St, has a flint and stone Norman tower, and an impressive collection of Tudor monuments.

A path from the church leads to **Denham Court**, dating back to the 17th century, where Charles II went into hiding after the Battle of Worcester. But the grandest house in the village is **Denham Place**, built for Sir Roger Hill in 1688. It is situated behind the long brick wall at the green, across the bridge over the River Misbourne at the other end of the main street from the church. Denham Place was the former home of Lord Vansittart, who, as Under Secretary of State at the Foreign Office in the 1930s, spoke out against then Prime Minister Neville Chamberlain's appeasement policy.

Moated **Savay Farm**, a 15-minute walk from the village green, across the railway and fields, dates back to the 14th century. It was also the wartime home, after his release from internment, of the Blackshirt fascist leader Sir Oswald Mosley, whose wife Cynthia was buried in the grounds.

DINTON

Map p.145, A2 ★
2 miles NE of Haddenham off the A418

A compact village on a low, limestone ridge above the River Thame, Dinton has a narrow High St of brick, stone, timber-framed and thatched cottages, and a large, thatched farmhouse in the middle of the village at Westlington Farm. The hamlet of **Westlington**, a picturesque cluster of whitewashed, thatched cottages around a small green, is joined to Dinton at its south-east corner.

🏠 **Glebe House**, in a large, terraced garden opposite the church, is the tallest building built from witchert in the county (see HADDENHAM). A small green below Dinton's church is overlooked by a row of brick and stone cottages. 'The Summers' is a pair of timber-framed cottages, with brick infill, that were originally one house; their blocked fireplaces can still be seen in the gable walls. There are wooden stocks on the green, with another set hanging in the church porch.

⛪ The **Church of St Peter and St Paul** is approached up a cobbled path between overhanging yews and makes an impressive sight on the skyline when climbing the hill from the south. It has a long, 13th-century nave and chancel, with a large, castellated tower and stair turret. The chancel was extended and the interior restored in 1868 by G.E.Street, giving it a mainly Victorian appearance inside.

But there is still a magnificent Norman doorway on the south, which bears zigzag mouldings and a stone tympanum showing two dragons quarrelling over the Tree of Life. Below is a carved lintel depicting St Michael using a cross to fend off a third dragon. The font has a fluted lower part, possibly Norman, with 14th- and 15th-century carvings above. In addition there are a number of medieval brasses in the chancel, and a Jacobean pulpit.

🏠 **Dinton Hall** is a large, rambling house, partly hidden behind a high wall beside the churchyard. The oldest part is stone-built, probably 14th-century, but all that can be seen from the lane is a long line of brick gables, steep, tiled roofs and tall brick chimneys. The south front, altered in the 18th and 19th century, is almost invisible from the road. The house was once home to the Mayne family, whose most famous scion, Simon, was a judge at Charles I's trial – 'a great committee man,' according to one report, 'where-in he licked his fingers.' His servant, who was alleged to have been the king's executioner, eventually became a recluse known as the 'Dinton hermit' whose main preoccupation was the patching of his clothes. By the time he died, in 1696, he had acquired a gargantuan carapace of rags and shoes that had swollen to 10 times their original size. One of these monsters, comprising more than 1,000 pieces of leather, can be found in Oxford's Ashmolean Museum.

The Castle is an attractively ruined hunk of masonry that stands by the roadside near the green. It was built in 1769 by Sir John Vanhatten, of Dinton Hall, to serve both as an eye-catching folly and as a home for his fossil collection. However, while most follies were intended to have an air of romantic decay, this one has become rather more dilapidated than its creator intended.

At **Ford**, a hamlet in the parish of Dinton, a lane leads to Moat Farm past the small, stone pub and an attractive group of white rendered, thatched cottages. On the other side of the Dinton road, another lane passes more stone and thatch cottages and large, red brick farmhouses at Ford Farm and Manor Farm. There are footpaths across the low-lying meadows east of the village to the isolated Moreton Farm, where the former village of Moreton once stood.

DORNEY

Map p.142, D2
3 miles NW of Eton on the B3026

The village stands in a tiny southern pocket of Buckinghamshire, facing water

meadows that lead down to the Thames. Although close to the M4, Dorney has contrived to protect itself, as it has for centuries, from almost anything that might change its essentially Tudor character: even the small amount of housing put up this century is half-timbered and set well away from older buildings. Dorney Court (see p.18 and picture, p.68) is to the west of the village.

St James' Church has a Norman nave, with a 14th-century chancel and a castellated Tudor tower. The interior contains a Norman font and some fine brasses, along with 17th-century box pews and monuments.

DORTON

Map p.148, F4
3 miles NE of Oakley on minor roads off the B4011

Dorton is a tiny hamlet, comprising its manor, **Dorton House**, with its own church and a few estate cottages all built in the grounds. Dorton House itself, a red-brick mansion built in 1626 and altered 150 years later, was once the seat of the Aubreys, baronets of Boarstall. It is now the home of Ashfold Preparatory School. St John's Church, alongside, is built of stone rubble with a weather-boarded bell turret. It serves as a chapel for the school.

There is little more to say about Dorton; yet two sad stumps of masonry in the nearby Dorton Wood might have told a different story. They are all that remains from a 19th-century attempt to make Dorton a spa to rival Cheltenham and Bath. Hoping to exploit the supposedly curative qualities of the sulphurous, inky water from the wood's chalybeate spring, developers in the 1830s built a domed and pillared pumphouse modelled on the Tower of Winds at Athens, set in acres of landscape gardens. Queen Victoria herself prepared to take the waters there, and Dorton's future seemed assured.

But royal whim took the Queen to

Leamington instead, and Dorton languished. By the end of the century, the spa buildings were in ruins, and tranquillity prevailed. Today, the spring itself is a muddy pool and a well in a wooden hut covered with a plastic roof.

DRAYTON PARSLOW

Map p.149, A4
4 miles E of Winslow off the B4032

Drayton Parslow is a quiet village of about 200 houses, mostly brick but with some thatch, lining both sides of the B4032. Set in a swathe of farm land south of Milton Keynes, it stands on a ridge overlooking the Ouzel Valley. The name Parslow comes from the Passelaw family, lords of the manor for several generations from the reign of Henry I. In the 17th century, Drayton Parslow was well-known for a foundry where church bells were cast; many are still in use today, over at least six counties.

The mainly 18th-century **Holy Trinity Church** still has traces of its 12th-century origins visible. Inside the Victorian interior, a 15th-century alabaster panel above the altar depicts the crucifixion. There is also an octagonal font with an unusual castellated rim.

DUNTON

Map p.149, C4
3 miles NE of Whitchurch off the A418

An obscure hamlet north of CUBLINGTON and WHITCHURCH, Dunton has a church, an early 18th-century rectory, a manor farm and a few cottages.

St Martin's Church is a much altered building with red-brick dressings on stone on the outside. A Norman doorway leads to a restored Norman nave and a late Georgian interior, in which oak beams reach up to a whitewashed ceiling with a west gallery. There are several portrait

brasses, some of which date from as long ago as 1420.

EDGCOTT

Map p.148, C3
3 miles SW of Steeple Ashton off the A41

A small village with a church and two old farm houses, Edgcott is sandwiched between the brickworks at Calvert and Grendon prison. It looks down from a slope across fields which run to the A41 and off towards BRILL.

Rectory Farm is a 17th-century timber-framed building and the 18th-century Manor Farm has chequered brickwork on a stone base.

St Michael's Church is small but exquisitely formed. Its west tower, nave and chancel are a mixture of 14th- and 15th-century building; some of the pews date back to the 16th century.

EDLESBOROUGH

Map p.151, D1
3 miles NW of Ivinghoe off the A4146

The village, clustered around its church, consists mostly of modern housing, but it does have one or two period buildings, including a 200-ft-long 16th-century tithe barn at Church Farm and a 19th-century windmill (now sail-less) that looks north from the village across the Bedfordshire border.

Edlesborough's most impressive building is **St Mary's Church**. Mostly dating from the 14th century, the church has a castellated tower and roof, now minus its spire, which was destroyed by lightning in 1828.

Inside, the treasures include a 15th-century hourglass-shaped pulpit and a number of medieval wood carvings in the rood screen and choir seats. There is a full-size effigy in brass of a 14th-century knight,

The Chinese Room, Claydon House, Middle Claydon

Sir John de Swynesteade, and a 15th-century rose brass in the chancel. A Tudor fireplace is set high up in the wall of the north aisle.

The nearby hamlet of **Northall**, which falls into the parish of Edlesborough, is reputed to be haunted by the ghost of highwayman Dick Turpin, who allegedly preyed on coaches travelling the road between Tring and Dunstable. It is said that a blocked window at nearby Butler's Manor was his spying point.

ELLESBOROUGH

Map p.146, B1
3 miles NE of Princes Risborough off the A4010

The village (picture, p.73) is little more than a small cluster of cottages grouped around a church where a bend in the road cuts into the wooded slopes beneath Cymbeline's Mount (picture, p.57), the site of a motte-and-bailey castle. The low almshouses, south of the church, were built in 1746.

The **Church of St Peter and St Paul**, on a mound beside the road, is mainly Victorian on the outside, following extensive restoration between 1854 – 1871. It has a tall, castellated, south west tower and stair-turret built of flint. The interior is late 14th-century with octagonal stone piers forming the south arcade. There is an alabaster monument to Bridget Croke (d.1638).

There are several 16th- and 17th-century houses in the low-lying meadows to the north of the village, many of which are moated. **Terrick House**, built in 1702, is on the Lower Icknield Way, a mile to the north east.

A mile further on is **Stoke House**, one of the best houses of its period in the county, on the edge of Stoke Mandeville. It was built in 1700 of reddish brown brick with a carved wooden cornice and a doorcase which includes a shell canopy. A little further on is Moat Farm, an L-shaped 16th-century farmhouse. The same stream feeds the moats at the farm and Stoke House.

Chequers, in the parish of Ellesborough, is on the Chiltern escarpment above the village. The house, originally 16th-century, is now famous as the official country residence of Prime Ministers, of whom Lloyd George was the first to enjoy the privilege, and consequently for security reasons it is very much closed to the public. It was donated to the nation in 1917 by Lord Lee of Fareham, following substantial alterations in 1912 by the architect Sir Reginald Blomfield.

The house is now an attractive mixture of patterned red brick and stone with mullioned windows, gabled roofs and clusters of tall chimneys. There is a walled garden on the south side, facing a long avenue that is crossed by the Ridgeway path. The path originally ran much closer to the house, but was diverted to improve security. Even so, it is difficult to walk the path through the grounds without experiencing the unnerving sensation of being watched.

EMBERTON

Map p.156, F2
1 mile S of Olney off the A509

Emberton lies in the lush valley of the Great Ouse, now by-passed by the A509 Newport Pagnell to Olney road. Since no other road from the village actually leads anywhere, the only reason for going to this quiet little backwater is to visit the place.

The focal point of the village is the clock tower, donated by the Reverend Thomas Fry in 1846 in memory of Margaret, the second of his three wives. The clock tower was restored in 1972. Immediately to the north of the village is the entrance to Emberton Country Park (see p.25).

All Saints' Church at the south end of the village, built in the late 14th century, was considerably restored – arguably over-restored – in Victorian times. The list of parish rectors displayed in the entrance to the church includes the name of Samuel Pepys MA (1664), unsung namesake of the celebrated contemporary diarist. The church is said to house the remains of the unfortunate Sir Everard Digby, one of the Gunpowder Plot conspirators, who lived at nearby GAYHURST.

FARNHAM COMMON

Map p.142, C3
3 miles N of Slough off the A 355

Farnham Common is mostly a large post-war housing estate on the edge of Burnham Beeches (see BURNHAM). There is a small church, St John's, built in 1907. The large private house Yew Place has parts dating back to the time of King John, and one modern dwelling of note, the curiously named **Egypt End**, a striking piece of 1930s modernist architecture built from concrete with spiral iron staircases inside and out.

Prolific children's author Enid Blyton and J.M. Barrie, the creator of Peter Pan, are among the famous names who have stayed in the area. The village is also home to the Moore family from which three generations have competed for Britain in the Olympic Games.

Farnham Royal, strung out along the road a further mile towards Slough, has effectively become a continuation of its large neighbour. Its origins, though, are ancient. It earned the right to call itself Royal from William the Conqueror, who gave the honour of providing a glove for his coronation to Farnham's lord of the manor. St Mary's Church, much restored in the 19th century, has a Norman chancel.

FAWLEY

Map p.140, B4
6 miles W of Marlow off the A4155

The village is isolated amongst steep beech woods, approached along narrow lanes on a ridge above the Thames valley. There is a small green with an old well, but most of the houses are hidden from the road in mature gardens. Fawley House, built in

1740, replaced an earlier rectory. At the north end of the village is the 18th-century Roundhouse Farm, part of which, as its name suggests, is circular in plan with a conical roof.

There are good walks from the farm, through Great Wood, towards HAMBLEDEN or north-west towards Stonor in Oxfordshire. Fawley Court (see p.18) is two miles to the south, beside the River Thames.

St Mary's Church stands beside a pond in a graveyard overhung with trees. It has a late 13th-century tower, added to in the 16th century, but the remainder, apart from the chancel which was rebuilt in 1748, is the product of extensive restoration in 1883. The carved pulpit and lectern are 17th-century and there is a large monument to Justice Sir James Whitelock (d.1632). There is a domed mausoleum of 1750 for the Freemans in the churchyard, and another of 1862 for the Mackenzie family.

FENNY STRATFORD

Map p.154, F3
3 miles SE of Central Milton Keynes on the B4034

Fenny Stratford, on the old Roman road of Watling Street, merges imperceptibly with its near neighbour BLETCHLEY to the west, and both are now part of the new straggling city of MILTON KEYNES. Fenny Stratford's main claim to fame is linked to a curious tradition of its church: the Fenny Poppers.

St Martin's Church, at the junction of Watling St and Aylesbury St, was built in the 1720s by Dr Browne Willis, a noted antiquary and sometime MP for Buckingham. By coincidence, both his father and grandfather had died on St Martin's Day – 11 November – while his grandfather had lived and died in St Martin's Lane in London. Hence Browne Willis's choice of the name for his new church. He decreed that a special service should be held at the church each St Martin's Day and, somewhat more bizarre, that six pieces of ordnance he had donated

63

to the church – the Fenny Poppers – should be fired in a nearby field. Browne Willis's request is still honoured: on 11 November each year, the sound of gunfire is heard throughout Fenny Stratford (and even, or so it is said, as far away as Olney, some 12 miles distant).

The church has since been enlarged (in 1866, 1908 and 1965) and Browne Willis's original building now forms the north aisle. Its benefactor died a poor man in 1760, and is buried within the church, which still houses his Fenny Poppers.

FINGEST

Map p.140, B4 ★
6 miles NW of Marlow on minor roads off the B482

The village, smaller now than it was in the 18th century, is at the meeting point of three valleys, with steep wooded slopes. Its timber-framed and brick cottages are grouped around two sides of a large churchyard. The open fields beyond the church were the site of a palace belonging to the Bishops of Lincoln. Some larger houses have twin-gabled roofs, including the Chequers Inn, with its symmetrical red and blue, chequered-pattern brick frontage and flint gable walls. The Old Rectory is a pleasant, brick-fronted house opposite the churchyard. There are good views over the village above Manor Farm, from Hanger Wood, down the broad Hambleden valley.

⛪ The most striking feature of **St Bartholomew's Church**★(picture, p.81) is its imposing Norman tower, which seems too massive for the rest of the church, built of flint with stone quoining and rough rendered. The tower has paired, round-headed bell openings on all four sides and a twin saddleback roof that was probably added in the 17th century. It may have been used as the original nave before the 13th-century chancel was built. The narrow, plain interior, over-restored in 1866, includes an octagonal 14th-century font.

At **Fingest Grove**, along a narrow lane north-east of the village, there is an attractive group of cottages and farm buildings overlooking a small green. A flint house with brick dressings occupies the middle of the group. It has a chequered brick upper storey, central bay and mullioned windows. **Skirmet**, a hamlet of colour-washed, timber-frame and brick cottages in the Hambleden valley, is half a mile to the south

⚲ The 17th-century **Old Crown** pub in Skirmet was originally three separate cottages, one the village shop. It has a white painted tap room and large inglenook fireplace. The mid 19th-century church is now a private house.

FRIETH

Map p.141, A1
4 miles NW of Marlow off the B482

The village, deep in the Chilterns, is a mixture of flint cottages, Victorian houses and some more modern buildings, most of which are arranged along a single street. The Old Parsonage, built in 1869, is a red-brick, gabled house set in a large garden, opposite the village school and hall. There is a group of restored farm buildings at the western end.

⛪ The **Church of St John the Evangelist**, in the middle of the village, was built in 1848 as a chapel of ease for HAMBLEDEN, less than three miles to the south, where the parish church presides. Local farmers carted wagonloads of flints from the ruined wing of the Old Rectory at Hambleden for the construction of the new church. It was later enlarged by adding a south aisle in 1872 and has a simple interior, enlivened by wood panelling in the chancel, with colourful stained glass.

A narrow lane to the south winds towards Hambleden, keeping to the high ground above the valley. It passes **Little Parmoor**, a group of 17- and 18th-century buildings

Milton's Cottage, Chalfont St Giles

including a large, red-brick house and smaller cottages of flint with brick dressings. There is a small cluster of farm buildings further south at **Rockwell End** and a larger hamlet of red-brick houses set in large gardens at **Pheasant's Hill**, clinging to the side of the broad Hambleden valley.

FULMER

Map p.142, B4
4 miles N of Slough off the B416

In a snug hollow by the River Alderbourne, Fulmer has retained its charm despite the alarming proximity of the M25 and M4, which intersect less than a mile away. Its houses are a mixture of ages, mostly 18th- and 19th-century and brick-built; they blend so well together that they might have been selected for the purpose.

St James's Church, built in 1610 by Sir Marmaduke Dayrell, the Lord of the Manor, stands at the village crossroads. It was only the second church built in England after the Reformation, although it retains traces of its predecessor, including its 15th-century doorway. Inside is a handsome, canopied monument to Sir Marmaduke, in armour with his wife beside him and their children kneeling at their feet. Having fought for Queen Elizabeth, he went on to become treasurer both to James I and Charles I, as his inscription explains, 'employed in matters of great trust for the space of 50 years.'

GAWCOTT

Map p.152, F4
1½ miles SW of Buckingham off the A421

Gawcott village lies in rolling north Buckinghamshire countryside, its predominantly brick buildings curled around Main St from which run three different roads to Buckingham and its outskirts. A quiet, placid place that still retains a school and a pub, its main claim to fame is as the birthplace of the Victorian

Gothic architect Sir George Gilbert Scott.

His father was both architect and vicar of Gawcott's Holy Trinity church by the sharp bend in Main St. The church is of no great note; Scott's interest in architecture was apparently inspired by the church at HILLESDEN two miles to the south.

Scott went on to become professor of architecture at the Royal Academy and was credited with building or restoring 474 churches (including that at Hillesden) 38 cathedrals and around 200 other buildings. His most famous work is London's St Pancras Station.

Radclive, a mile and a half to the north, is a tiny hamlet on the banks of the Great Ouse. Its Church of St John the Evangelist is medieval but was extensively restored in 1903, although it retained its early 12th-century southern doorway. Some of its stained glass is 14th-century. Close to the church is the **Grange**, a private manor house at one time owned by New College, Oxford. It is the surviving part of a larger Elizabethan building.

GAYHURST

Map p.154, B2
2 miles NW of Newport Pagnell on the B526

The only evidence of Gayhurst on the main B526 is the Sir Francis Drake pub (on the left-hand side, heading north). Immediately to one side of the pub a narrow lane leads through open park and grazing land with a small lake on the left. Half-a-mile-or-so up the lane, a notice beside a gate and cattle grid proclaims that the land thereafter is 'strictly private' property. This is Gayhurst. For, like its near neighbour TYRINGHAM, there is no village of Gayhurst: just the grounds and estate of a private house. In the case of Gayhurst, though, the church is included within the bounds of the private estate, accessible via a public footpath from the cattle grid.

Gayhurst House, externally a splendid example of Elizabethan grandeur, was built in 1597, and was once owned by Sir Everard Digby, a Catholic who was hanged, drawn and quartered for his part in the Gunpowder Plot of 1605. He pledged £1,500 towards the doomed cause and Gayshurst became the forum where Guy Fawkes and other conspirators met to formulate their plan.

A profusion of anchors on the gateposts and around the house reflects the success of Everard's heir, Sir Kenelm Digby, who rose to become commissioner of the navy in Charles I's reign. The house was subsequently sold to George Wrighte in 1704 and underwent considerable alterations in both the 18th and 19th centuries. Of this modernizing programme came two good things: the grounds' landscaping by Capability Brown; and the erection of St Peter's Church in 1728.

♙ The **Church of St Peter**, adjacent to Gayhurst House and within the estate perimeter, is an outstanding example of the Classical style and a welcome relief from the medieval churches which dominate this part of the county. Commonly attributed to Wren – although work started four years after his death – it stands serenely in mature parkland, its fanciful cupola echoing the curving gables of Gayhurst's southern façade. The interior is a cool and graceful exposition of neo-classicism, which includes memorial statues to Sir Nathan Wright and his son, the first English commission for the diminutive French artist Louis-Francois Roubiliac – 'the great little Mr. Roubiliac' as one contemporary called him.

GERRARDS CROSS

Map p.142, A4
4 miles E of Beaconsfield off the A40

Set around a well-planted common with a pond, Gerrards Cross is the suburban dream come true: the archetypal dormitory suburb, where the streets are clean, the lawns are cut and every home is its owner's castle.

Since the coming of the railway it has sprouted new houses in every conceivable style, from mock-medieval, through mock-Georgian and Gothic to mock-American.

Large, imposing, and often quite beautiful, they sit amid overflowing gardens striving desperately to be unique. In a way they succeed; certainly they must be very comfortable to live in. But the accumulation of so much individuality lends the town a shapeless feel. It is easy to lose oneself among its tree-lined streets and easier still to drive into neighbouring CHALFONT ST PETER without realising it.

GREAT BRICKHILL

Map p.150, A3
4 miles E of Newton Longville off the A5

A straggling village on the Bedfordshire border south of the line of the Roman Watling Street, Great Brickhill is characterized by the brown stone used for its church and 18th-century houses. Its position on a high ridge, 500 ft above sea level, proved attractive to Oliver Cromwell, who stationed his troops here for six weeks during his march on Northampton from Aylesbury. **Cromwell's Cottage** still stands in the village and is a listed building. The country house **Stockgrove**, built in 1929 by W.Curtis Green is situated one mile south east of the village. A two-storey neo-Georgian building, it is set in a large country park.

♙ **St Mary's Church** has a 13th-century tower and turret, and a 15th-century south aisle. It was restored in the 18th century and its roofs were elevated in 1867. Inside are some 18th-century tablets commemorating the Burton family.

GREAT HAMPDEN

Map p.146, D2   ★
3 miles W of Great Missenden on minor roads off the A413

Sheltered behind high beechwoods in a quiet corner of the Chilterns, the village is little more than a hamlet, with its church half a mile away in the grounds of Hampden House. The small group of brick or rendered cottages, some thatched, a pub

and a row of council houses overlook the village green and cricket pitch on the edge of a wooded common.

St Mary Magdalen Church★ occupies a pastoral setting amidst grazing livestock in gently sloping parkland. The church, with neatly pointed flint and stone walls, has a tall 13th- and 14th-century nave, side aisles and chancel with a slender, castellated tower on the south side. The interior is notable for its monuments to the Hampden family, including several 15th- to 16th-century brasses, and a large hanging monument to John Hampden (d.1643), who played a prominent part in the Parliamentary side of the Civil War.

As a churchyard inscription explains, 'For these lands in Stoke Mandeville John Hampden was assessed in 20s ship money levied by command of the king without authority of law on the 4th of August 1635. By resisting this claim of the king in legal strife he upheld the right of the people under the law and became entitled to grateful remembrance.' The monument inside the church depicts his death at the battle of Chalgrove Field. There are also some early Tudor benches with linenfold panelling and a cup-shaped font, partly Norman, with a 14th-15th century frieze.

Unfortunately, the church is usually locked when there is no service.

Hampden House, hidden from the church by a tree-lined avenue, is a mid-18th-century house in the Gothic style, combining stucco with chequered brick. There are parts of an earlier house still remaining, including the 14th-century King John's Tower, although the medieval roof in the Hall was originally from farm buildings at Great Kimble. The house is now a business centre.

The 16th-century Rectory, refaced in red brick in the 18th century, is a mile south-east of the church, at the end of one of the long avenues radiating from Hampden House. The park is crossed by several paths, some of which form an almost perfect square, with the village in one corner and the two opposite sides following the line of Grim's Ditch, where the remains of Saxon earthworks are clearly visible. The line of the ditch continues south to the woods above Bradenham, but is lost soon after leaving the park to the west of Lodge Wood, to reappear in the woods south-east of Wendover. The purpose of the earthworks has never been firmly established. They may have been a defensive line or simply formed a boundary; it is not even certain whether the various sections were ever linked. The village is a good centre for woodland walks, including one to Whiteleaf Cross (see WHITELEAF) two miles to the north-west.

The mid 17th-century smock mill at **Lacey Green** (see p.29) is accessible by a footpath.

GREAT HORWOOD

Map p.149, A2
2 miles N of Winslow on minor roads

A a compact village on the edge of Whaddon Chase, Great Horwood dates back at least 1,200 years when Anglo-Saxon chronicles recorded 10 dwellings in 'Horwudu'. It is still a very small place, with a few Jacobean cottages and an 18th-century pub, the Crown Inn. During World War II, RAF Bomber Command had a Group Headquarters here and the skies throbbed with heavy aircraft. The former base is now a housing estate.

The 14th-century St James's Church has a modern roof above a 15th-century arcade; there are some fine carvings. The 15th-century Archbishop of Canterbury, William Warham, was once rector here.

GREAT KIMBLE

Map p.146, B1
2 miles NE of Princes Risborough on the A4010

Under the steep, wooded slopes of the Chiltern ridge, a few flint cottages and

Dorney Court, Dorney

some larger houses, including the Tudor-style Vicarage of 1859, occupy a short lane that links the Upper and Lower Icknield Way. The inn and church face each other across the lane where the village joins a noisy main road.

⛪ St Nicholas's Church, built of knapped flint with stone quoining, appears too grand for the size of the village. It has an attractive pattern of chequered flint and stone squares on the castellated nave and 14th-century west tower. The interior has narrow side aisles that continue either side of the chancel. These are separated from the nave by 13th-century octagonal piers. The chancel arch is 14th-century, but the chapels, originally of the same period, were rebuilt in 1876-81. There is a fine, cup-shaped, Norman font.

⛰ Ⓜ There is a fine view from **Pulpit Hill**, the site of an Iron Age fort. The hill can be seen from the churchyard rising above the dense, wooded slopes lining the Chiltern escarpment. The double rampart and ditch surrounding the fort are more prominent on the east side. There is another small fort at nearby **Ragpit Hill** with a single rampart and ditch on a natural spur. The forts are connected by the Ridgeway path, which passes within half a mile of the village.

GREAT LINFORD

Map p.154, C2
2 miles N of Central Milton Keynes off the A422

The Grand Union Canal turns through 90 degrees at Great Linford, and so this old village, now a suburb of the new city of MILTON KEYNES, is bounded by the canal both to the north and to the east. As with MILTON KEYNES VILLAGE and other ancient localities, it has been all but absorbed by new development. Yet it has managed to retain much of its character and, strolling through the delightful Linford Manor Park, or along the towpath of the Grand Union Canal, it is hard to imagine that it is part of a burgeoning new city whose glass-faced business and

shopping centres are barely ten minutes' drive away.

To the north of both the Grand Union Canal and the Great Ouse beyond is the smaller settlement of **Little Linford**. The Domesday Book of 1086 records them as one entity, under the name of Linforde, but the two evolved as separate communities. Access to Great Linford village is via Marlborough St or Monks Way (respectively V8 and H3 on the Milton Keynes grid system), both of which lead on to St Leger Drive. Off St Leger Drive either Parkside or Marsh Drive and then High St lead to alternative entrances to Linford Manor Park.

The Manor House itself, fronting directly onto the park with no surrounding wall or fence, was built in 1678 by Sir William Pritchard, Lord Mayor of London, as his principal country seat. Together with the neighbouring five acres of parkland, the house was acquired in 1972 by the Milton Keynes Development Corporation. Although the house and its immediate garden have since been returned to private ownership, the park remains a public amenity for the people of Milton Keynes.

⛪ The 13th-century **Church of St Andrew** lies within the bounds of Linford Manor Park. It was restored at the same time the Manor was built, but much good taste was swept away by Gothicization in 1884. However, traces of its former glory can still be discerned.

Adjoining it is a terrace of stone almshouses and a school house, all built on the instructions of Sir William Pritchard for the benefit of the villagers of Great Linford. The almshouses and school house, together with a renovated thatched barn, now combine to provide an arts centre and workshop, incorporating the **Barn Theatre**.

♣ Linford Valley Park is to the north of Great Linford High St, while to the south is a village cricket green and pavilion. To the east of Marsh Drive is Great Linford Park, effectively a continuation of Linford Valley Park. Here, a walk southwards along the bridleway beside the canal will bring you to The Dell, the site of restored kilns where bricks were made as long ago as 1679.

GREAT MISSENDEN

Map p.146, D3
4 miles W of Chesham on the A4128

Dating from Saxon times, the village of Great Missenden gets its name from the River Misbourne and the word 'dene', meaning a wooded valley. Some of the woods are still there, as is the valley and the Misbourne. But Great, nowadays, does little more than distinguish it from the smaller settlement of LITTLE MISSENDEN, about a mile to the south-east.

Although it has developed in recent years into quite a sizeable community, Great Missenden's heyday seems to have passed. The Misbourne, which once served a number of water mills along the valley, is reduced here to little more than a stream hidden beneath a culvert. And the High St, which at one time housed a dozen coaching inns, has become a traffic-clogged highway – despite the nearby A413 by-pass – with pavements that at one point are inadequate for two people walking abreast.

Despite the number of potentially interesting half-timbered buildings, the village is generally very ordinary and quite shabby, without the character one finds in many old village high streets. At the northern end, set back behind some shops on the western side, is a white-painted Baptist Church from the 1830s, looking rather like an over-sized mausoleum. To the south, meanwhile, Church St leads to Missenden Abbey and the parish church.

The 14th-century **Church of St Peter and St Paul** stands outside the village and is reached via a specially constructed bridge over the A413. It has an array of gargoyles on its tower and roof, a Norman font and some fine monuments.

Missenden Abbey – on the village side of the by-pass – is now owned and operated by Buckinghamshire County Council as a residential, adult education centre. Founded in 1133, the Abbey hosted King Henry III on at least five occasions between 1238 and 1256, and was re-endowed in 1293. It passed into private ownership after the Dissolution of the Monasteries and in 1810 was rebuilt in Gothic style. Much of it was destroyed by fire in 1985, but only three years later the restored Missenden Abbey was formally re-opened by the Duke of Gloucester.

GRENDON UNDERWOOD

Map p.148, D4
4 miles NW of Waddesdon off the A41

A long, narrow village on the old London–Stratford road, Grendon Underwood has close associations with William Shakespeare. According to the 17th-century writings of Sir John Aubrey, the playwright often stayed at what was then the Ship Inn and took inspiration from Grendon's two village constables for the characters Dogberry and Verges in *Much Ado About Nothing*. Other villagers were supposed to have been the basis for characters in *A Midsummer Night's Dream*. The 16th- and 17th-century timber-frame and brick building of the former inn is now **Shakespeare Farm**, off Main Road at the north-west end of the village. The inn's sign is now in the keeping of the Buckinghamshire Archaeological Society in Aylesbury.

St Leonard's Church, at the north end of Main Road, has recently suffered a severe attack of deathwatch beetle, prompting the complete restoration of all its pews. The church has a 13th-century nave, a 15th-century tower and a pulpit dated 1620. There is an effigy dated 1751 of John Piggott of Doddershall and his son, and marble monuments to Lord and Lady Saye and Sele.

Half a mile to the north of the village is the psychiatric unit of Grendon maximum security prison, built in grounds formerly belonging to Grendon Hall. Springhill Open Prison is located in the same grounds.

HADDENHAM

Map p.145. BI   ★★
5 miles NW of Princes Risborough off the A4129

The large, medieval village of Haddenham is set in the low lying Vale of Aylesbury, close to the River Thame. It is a delight to stroll through its narrow lanes or pass the time quietly by the pond beside the church. The village has grown in recent years to the size of a small town, yet has no recognizable centre; instead, it is a collection of 'ends', from Church End in the south to Town End in the north. The 'ends' were originally small hamlets or groups of houses whose inhabitants were all engaged in the same craft or trade and lived a more or less self-contained existence.

The west side of the village is defined by Townside, a winding lane that still connects several farms. Church Way used to define the east side and the heart of the village is found between these two streets. It is a maze of small lanes lined with stone and rendered cottages, including many built of witchert, a local material made from chalk marl mixed with straw. In essence, it is a kind of mud walling, built up in layers, usually rendered over, and is widely used throughout the village, in particular on garden walls where pantiles are sometimes used for copings. Wichert was dug from a mile-wide band of hard earth that stretches from LONG CRENDON to AYLESBURY and is peculiar to this part of the country.

The **High St** is just one of the maze of narrow lanes in the middle of the village. It includes the 17th-century Dove House, which has a dovecote, and Bone House, built in 1807 and decorated with the knuckle-bones of sheep. The top of the High St begins at Fort End, a small triangle of houses at a bend in the old road from Aylesbury to Thame, two miles to the south over the Oxfordshire border. On the south side of the village, in Gibson Lane, is Skittles Green, another 'end', where there

is one of the most attractive groups of cottages in the village. Flint St, originally called Duck Lane, was inhabited by duck breeders, and the brook that runs through the village once connected old duck-rearing ponds.

The focal point of the village, however, is **Church End**. It is a large green lined with rows of stone, rendered and thatched cottages behind neat gardens, with a church and village pond, complete with duck house. Church Farm House, on the east side of the church, has a 14th-century, stone built lower floor and a jettied, 15th-century, timber-framed upper floor. Grenville Manor, further on, is a rough stone built house of 1569 with a later, carved timber porch. In Church Way there is the stone built Green Dragon inn. The Old Vicarage is tucked out of sight with a small cluster of stone cottages in the north east corner of the green. Manor Farm House, west of the church, has a distinctive twin-gabled roof. It stands in a garden overlooking a farmyard of stone or weatherboarded barns and outbuildings, on the edge of open fields.

St Mary's Church sits in a churchyard whose walls contain one side of the duck pond. It has a large, 13th-century nave, side aisles and chancel, and a 15th-century north chapel. Its 13th-century west tower, built in the local limestone, is decorated at the top with blank arcading. It has a simple, spacious interior with a tall chancel arch. The carved Norman font has a frieze of dragons above a fluted bowl. The timber screens in the north side chapel and beneath the tower, and some of the pews, are 16th-century. There is some 15th-century stained glass in the chapel.

HAMBLEDEN

Map p.141, BI   ★★
4 miles W of Marlow off the A4155

The village (picture, p.86) lies in a steep valley, overlooked by beech woodland. It is

Ellesborough

approached over a small bridge across a stream which skirts the southern edge of the village. From here there is a distant view across meadows towards the River Thames. Hambledon has a small central square of reddish-brown brick and flint houses round a single chestnut tree, with a stone cross and a village pump. Rows of cottages with gabled dormers and a red brick, Victorian pub, the Stag and Huntsman, line a short street on the east side of the churchyard.

⛪ St Mary's Church★★ is approached through a gabled lich-gate, between clipped yew trees. The handsome tower of flint and red brick was built at the west end in 1721 after the Norman tower, centred over the original 11th-century church, had collapsed in 1703. Four corner turrets were added in 1883. The barn-like nave was rebuilt in the 13th century when the north transept was extended and an east aisle was added. The Lady Chapel, part of extensive restoration work in 1859, was converted from a 'sheepfold', so called because the farm labourers would attend services in their working clothes and the floor was strewn with straw. The chancel arch and the timber, panelled porch are also Victorian. There is some fine Early Renaissance panelling, said to have come from The Vyne in Hampshire, and a cylindrical Norman font.

A painted alabaster monument to Sir Cope d'Oyley (d.1633) and his family includes ten kneeling children, five sons and five daughters. The political sympathies of the sons, who fought on opposing sides in the Civil War, are shown by their dress, while those children holding a skull pre-deceased their father. There is a mid-18th-century, domed mausoleum for the Kenrick family on the north side of the churchyard, from where the complicated pattern of the church's plain tiled roofs and gables can best be seen; the churchyard also offers uninterrupted views up the Hambleden valley.

⛪ The early 17th-century Manor House, approached via a sweeping drive around a large copper beech, has a triple gabled front of flint with red brick dressings and brick

mullioned windows. The Rectory, which lies outside the village, was built in 1724 on the site of an earlier manor house.

Less than a mile to the south, where the Hambleden valley meets the Thames, is **Mill End★**, a picturesque group of houses consisting of the white-painted, timber-boarded Hambleden Mill itself, the Mill House and Mill End Farm (picture, p,76). The Marlow–Henley road passes close to the river, which can be glimpsed tantalizingly through the trees, but there is nowhere for motorists to stop. The mill is best approached by footpath, either from Hambleden or from the water meadows on the southern, Berkshire side of the river: there is a weir with a footbridge just opposite the mill

THE HALE

Map p.146, B3
2 miles E of Wendover off the A413

Set in a secluded location, at the head of a small valley, The Hale is a picturesque group of buildings comprising an irregular, rendered and red-brick house of 1743, a half-timbered farmhouse and several weatherboarded barns, now converted to private dwellings. There are broad vistas to the west, over fields of grazing sheep, to the tree-lined spur of Boddington Hill, where there is a hill fort. A narrow, sunken lane, cut into the chalk, winds up the steep hill through Hale Wood, where it meets Grim's Ditch (see GREAT HAMPDEN) and crosses the Ridgeway path. Wendover Woods, which cover the escarpment north of The Hale, have a network of marked forest walks.

HANSLOPE

Map p.153, B3
5 miles NW of Milton Keynes on minor roads off the A508

Hanslope has grown more into a small town than a village in recent years, largely as the result of the development of nearby MILTON KEYNES, which Hanslope serves as a commuter base. In the centre of the village on the northern edge of the Market Square stand **Horseshoe Cottages**, an unusual terrace of thatched stone cottages built in an arc.

🏠 The **Church of St James the Great** boasts one of the very few spires in the county. Built in 1250 and originally 205 ft high, it was struck by lightning in 1804. Even so, at 186 ft, the rebuilt version – constructed of Ketton stone – is certainly the tallest in Buckinghamshire, as well as one of the most distinctive: the octagonal, studded spire set atop a square tower is a landmark for miles around.

At its apex, from which it is said that seven counties may be viewed, there is a weathervane in the style of a whippet with an arrow through its paw. The studs at every angle of the spire are both decorative and functional, allowing access to free the vane if it stuck. One local vicar who performed this feat, shortly before the old spire was destroyed, became so elated that he had to be restrained from repeating his odyssey while drunk.

The churchyard's most famous resident is one Alexander McKay, a bare-knuckled prize-fighter and 'champion of all Scotland' who died in 1830, aged only 26, after a fight with Irishman Simon Byrne. Since prize-fighting was illegal, Byrne was charged with McKay's murder; the money and influence of the fight's backers ensured his acquittal.

More recently – on 21st July 1912, to be precise – Edward Watts, squire of Hanslope, was shot by his gamekeeper who then turned the gun on himself. The Watts family mansion, Hanslope Park (half a mile outside the village to the south-east), is now a communications centre owned and operated by the Foreign and Commonwealth Office.

HARDWICK

Map p.149, D3
3 miles N of Aylesbury off the A413

Laid out in a square pattern around a central green, Hardwick's attractions include a medieval church, a manor farm, a 16th-century rectory and the village pub, the Bell Inn.

🏠 The ancient **St Mary's Church** has a Saxon nave and some fine old glass from the 14th century. It is also the site of an unusual tomb, the resting place of 247 Civil War soldiers from both sides killed in a bloody skirmish at Holman's Bridge, near Aylesbury, in 1642 when Prince Rupert's Royalist troops engaged the Parliamentarians who held Aylesbury. The dead were buried in an unmarked grave in a field next to the bridge until they were discovered and re-interred in 1818; the tomb was erected by the local historian Lord Nugent, who lived at nearby Weedon. The church, which was restored in 1873, is also worth visiting for its pre-Norman nave and 14th-century tower. Inside is a monument to Sir Thomas Lee (an ancestor of Robert E. Lee, the American Civil War confederate leader), who had estates in Hardwick and Weedon and built Hartwell House near Aylesbury. Dated 1616, it features the figures of Sir Thomas, his wife and their 14 children.

HARTWELL

Map p.149, F3
2 miles SW of Aylesbury on the A418

The village, which is strictly speaking the twin tiny hamlets of Upper and Lower Hartwell, on the edge of Aylesbury in the parish of Stone, is dominated by **Hartwell House** and its grounds. The walls which surround them on the Oxford Road are embedded with ammonites, some of substantial size, and it is possible that these spiral fossils gave the name to The Bugle Horn, the old pub which stands on the bend in the road, opposite the entrance to the house.

Now an hotel, **Hartwell House** is closed to the public except as paying guests. Its rich history began in the early 1600s, when it was built for Sir Thomas Lee. In 1755, the house was modernized by Henry Keene for Sir William Lee, the fourth baronet, and the grounds

(including a curved lake) were laid out by Capability Brown. Half a century later, after Sir George Lee vacated Hartwell to take holy orders, the house became the temporary residence of Louis VIII, the exiled Bourbon king of France. A scholarly man, nicknamed 'the sage of Hartwell', Louis nevertheless wasted no time making internal alterations to accommodate the regal lifestyle of himself and his 150-strong entourage. In 1814 , after the abdication of Napoleon Bonaparte, he left Hartwell to take up the French throne.

In 1825 the Egyptologist Dr John Lee took up residence in his ancestral home. Evidence of his passion is apparent at the curious 'Egyptian spring' on the road to Lower Hartwell.

During World War II the house was requisitioned by the army, after which it became a girls' school until 1963, when a fire ravaged the interior, although most of the contents were saved. The house and grounds are now owned by the Ernest Cook Trust and leased to Historic House Hotels Ltd. Guests should note the grand carved staircase and the faces of Winston Churchill and G.K. Chesterton among the carvings.

✠ The **Church of the Assumption** opposite the house was built by Henry Keene in 1756 in the early Gothic Revival style. Now disused, it lay neglected and ruined for many years until restoration work was carried out by the Buckinghamshire Historic Churches Trust in the 1980s.

HEDGERLEY

Map p.142, B3
5 miles N of Slough on minor roads off the A355

Hedgerley is a little village tucked into chalk hills less than a mile south of the M40. Its main street has a mix of brick-and-tile and half-timbered cottages. There was a Roman settlement here, with pottery as a local industry, although from medieval times up to World War II the village was noted for its brick production.

✠ **St Mark's Church** is Victorian, on the site of a much older building, and containing many of its predecessor's adornments. A 17th-century painting in the church is worth seeing: an illustration of the ten commandments and the consequences of breaking them. One memorable scene shows Jezebel being eaten by wild dogs – the penalty for bearing false witness.

HIGH WYCOMBE

Map p.146, F2
13 miles S of Aylesbury on the A40

The town, which grew up during the 18th and 19th centuries around the furniture industry, is now the largest in Buckinghamshire. The initial impression, especially if you approach from the south or west, is of traffic roundabouts, supermarket carparks, pedestrian underpasses, a bus station and shopping precinct, but hidden behind the unwelcoming modern surface is the core of a small, 18th-century market town. The old Oxford-to-London road used to follow the south bank of the River Wye, where the roads from Marlow and Amersham cross the narrow Wye valley, making High Wycombe the region's principal market for corn, cloth and lace. Indeed, it was originally called Chepping Wycombe, ('Chipping' once meant 'market'), and markets are still held on Tuesdays, Fridays and Saturdays.

At the Cornmarket end of the broad High St is the **Guildhall**, built in 1757 by Henry Keene. It was a gift of Lord Shelburne, who was Prime Minister from 1782-83. The handsome, red-brick building is raised on an arcade of stone columns above an open ground floor. It was renovated in 1859 by Sir G. H. Dashwood. The Market House is in Church Square, opposite the Guildhall. It was rebuilt in 1761 from designs by Robert Adam, replacing the earlier Shambles built

Hambleden Mill, Hambleden

in 1604 on the site of the Hog Market. The semi-octagonal brick upper floor is supported on arched openings around an undercroft with projecting wings. The lantern and leaded roof were added at the end of the 19th century.

The 17th- and 18th-century houses lining the High St have been infilled with more modern buildings and in many instances spoilt by modern shop fronts. The former Red Lion inn, for example, has had the lower part of its façade replaced by an arcade to provide the frontage for Woolworths.

Not all has been lost. No. 30 retains a flint façade with red brick dressings, a timber cornice and Doric doorcase; No. 33 is built in a plum-coloured brick with rubbed brick dressings, a moulded cornice and stone balustraded parapet. No. 39 has a grey brick façade, with a pediment over its projecting central bay, and a Doric doorcase.

All Saints' Church, behind the market place, has a stone and brick chequered tower and a long nave and chancel of knapped flint with stone quoining. It is Norman in origin and once had a central tower, pulled down in 1509 when the present west tower was built. The upper part of the tower was added by Henry Keene in 1755. The body of the church was enlarged in 1275, but its appearance now owes much to extensive restoration in 1889.

The interior of the nave has the proportions of a large town church, with an open beamed roof and double arch below the tower, the upper part of which belonged to the original 13th-century window. The chancel has a barrel roof and side chapels. In the north chapel is the tomb of Henry Petty, Earl of Shelburne (d.1751), which is almost the full height of the church. It was sculpted in 1754 by Peter Scheemakers, who also produced the Shakespeare monument in Westminster Abbey.

On the north side of the churchyard is a steep path, Castle Place, which bridges the railway cutting to reach the **Wycombe Local History & Chair Museum**★ (see

p.30). The High St runs into Easton St at the opposite end to the Guildhall, where it passes the remains of the 12th-century Hospital, consisting of no more than a short length of wall that was once part of the original Royal Grammar School. Further on is the Rye, bordered on the north by the little River Wye and the London road. It originally formed part of lands belonging to St John's, but later became common land.

The annual Wycombe Show takes place on the Rye, when cattle, sheep and goats again return to the meadow. There is still a working water wheel on the River Wye. A model in the Local History Museum shows the original Pann Mill, one of six water-powered cornmills attached to the manor of Wycombe. At the west end of the Rye is Wycombe Abbey, built in 1795 by James Wyatt. Formerly the home of the Shelburne family, it is now a school. The view south is of the steep, wooded hillside lining the Wye valley.

High Wycombe Tourist Information Office: 0494 421892.

National Trust Regional Office (Thames & Chilterns): 0494 528051.

HILLESDEN

Map p.148, B4
5 miles W of Winslow on minor roads off the A413

Hillesden is a tiny hamlet, no more than a handful of cottages reached by a narrow lane from a very modest 'main' road. But it has an astonishing church.

All Saints' Church is the best example of the Perpendicular style in the county, and the boyhood inspiration of the Victorian architect Sir George Gilbert Scott (see GAWCOTT). The original 13th-century structure was rebuilt by monks at the end of the 15th century, and from outside, the entire building seems broad and sweeping, with its two castellated towers and deep windows. Inside, the narrowness of the arch pillars and the ranks of tall stained-glass panes (many of them 15th-century) combine to induce a soaring sensation in the beholder. There is a sketch on display made by Scott at the age of 15; as a grown man, and one of his country's most celebrated architects, he was responsible for the church's major restoration.

Bullet holes in the church door tell another story. In the Civil War, Hillesden was a royalist outpost sandwiched between the parliamentary strongholds of NEWPORT PAGNELL and AYLESBURY, and was the scene of some hard fighting. The cost included the destruction of Hillesden Hall, the great house that once stood beside All Saints'.

HOGGESTON

Map p.149, C3
3 miles SE of Winslow off the A413

There are still signs of the earthwork bank that during the Civil War provided a ring of defence for Hoggeston. The village has some white-painted and thatched cottages, a church and a Jacobean manor house to the south.

Holy Cross Church is Norman, with many evolutions and additions over the centuries. A stone monument inside shows a lying figure holding a little chapel, probably intended as a model of Holy Cross Church itself. The memorial is believed to be dedicated to a member of the de Bermingham family, who owned the manor for three hundred years from the 13th century.

HULCOTT

Map p.150, E2
3 miles NE of Aylesbury off the A418

A tiny village clustered around a large rectangular green, Hulcott has been comfortably bypassed by modern developments. Reached by a single lane which comes off and rejoins the A418 just outside BIERTON, the village consists of a church, a manor house, a farm house and a few cottages. Church Farmhouse is a 17th-century timber-framed building with an 18th-century brick front.

All Saints' Church is best approached through the 19th-century lich-gate to the south side. A stone and tiled building with 13th-century origins, it has a weatherboard bellcot with 16th-century timbers visible inside. The church contains a plain tomb, said to be of Benedict Lee, the Lord of the Manor, who died in 1547, and a brass monument to the Rev William Bonus of Buckland.

HYDE HEATH

Map p.146, D4
2 miles E of Great Missenden off the A413

The village of Hyde Heath is largely a product of the 20th century, but no less pleasant and attractive for that. Ordnance Survey maps of the latter part of the 19th-century show just a handful of houses and an inn around what is now the village common, plus a few outlying farms and scattered properties, with the eponymous heath itself about a mile to the north west of the present village, which is now a commuter settlement for nearby towns such as HIGH WYCOMBE, AYLESBURY and AMERSHAM.

Recent development has been almost exclusively to the south of the Common, which, until about 30 years ago, was covered in bracken and gorse. It is now well-tended lawn, with a children's play area and a cricket pitch and pavilion.

To the eastern end of the Common is the tiny Church of St Andrew, of unusually domestic appearance: built of brick and flint, it would be almost indistinguishable from nearby cottages but for the small cross on the roof-top above the door.

Prominent among the outlying properties is **Hyde House** (or Hyde Hall as it was known in the 19th century), at the end of a long, straight driveway leading directly from the Chesham–Great Missenden road. Isaac d'Israeli (1766-1848), a prominent figure in London literary circles, brought his family to live at

Hyde Hall in 1825, and it was here that his son, Benjamin Disraeli (1804–1881) – himself to become an eminent and prolific novelist and later prime minister, statesman and the first (and last) Earl of Beaconsfield – wrote his first novel, *Vivian Grey*, published in 1826.

IBSTONE

Map p.145, F2
2 miles S of Stokenchurch off the A40

The village is approached from STOKENCHURCH, to the north, through dense woodland bordering the Wormsley Estate with steep valleys glimpsed on either side through the trees. Strung out for a mile and a half along a narrow ridge of hills that drops towards FINGEST, a mile to the south, Ibstone has no real centre to speak of; its houses, ranging from early 19th- to mid 20th-century buildings, are frequently separated by expanses of open common or hidden behind tall hedges and garden walls.

A narrow side lane leads to the church, and Manor Farm, a 17th-century flint-and-brick house surrounded by weatherboarded outbuildings. To the west of Ibstone the 17th-century Wormsley Farm and 18th-century Wormsley House may be glimpsed across the valley from the footpath through Wormsley Park.

Set in a shady churchyard, the **Church of St Nicholas**★ stands on a spur with splendid views across the valley towards Turville Heath. It has a small bellcot, hung with wooden shingles, a nave and 13th-century chancel of rough rendered flint with stone dressings, a Norman south doorway and the remains of another arched doorway built into the north wall. The interior is simple, with whitewashed walls and an exposed timber roof. There are 13th-century windows in the chancel and a Norman tub font opposite the blocked north door. In Norman times, the font would most usually have been placed near this door, thus giving the devil a handy exit

from the church once he had been driven out by baptism – a fact which also explains why many people preferred not to be buried on the north side.

ICKFORD

Map p.144, B2
3 miles SW of Long Crendon off the A418

The village is best approached from the south, where water meadows lead to the Oxfordshire border at the River Thame and a double humpback bridge, built from stone and brick in 1685. There is an informal cluster of white-painted stone and half-timbered cottages, surrounded by low stone walls, close by the church, and another group by the Rising Sun pub. The Old Rectory, beside the church, has 16th-century stone and timber-framed wings, connected by a red-brick, central range that was added in the 19th century. There is a thatched woodshed in the garden. The Grange, on the other side of the lane, is a stone house in the Victorian Gothic style.

St Nicholas's Church sits in a large churchyard crowded with copper beech and yew trees. It is built of stone with a low, buttressed, 12th-century nave and taller, 13th-century chancel. The tower has a saddleback roof and twin bell openings all round. Inside there is a gallery at the west end, a 17th-century pulpit and a monument to Thomas Tipping (d.1595) with panels in low relief depicting nine children. There is a footpath from the churchyard, across open fields to WORMINGHALL.

ILMER

Map p.145, C2
3 miles NW of Princes Risborough off the A4129

The massive, brick arch carrying the railway line between High Wycombe and Bicester provides a curiously grand approach to this tiny village, at the end of a

Fingest Church

narrow lane off the road from Princes Risborough to Thame.

⛪ St Peter's Church is stone built, with a 12th-century nave and 13th-century chancel. The weatherboarded bell turret has a shingled spire which was added in 1890. It has a dark, simple interior. The chancel screen, which sits on a low, stone wall, is medieval. There are carvings at the base of the north window in the chancel, depicting the Trinity and St Christopher. The church, which was restored by G.E.Street in 1859-60, is also the parish church for the nearby hamlet of **Longwick**.

At **Owlswick** there is a hamlet of white rendered and red brick houses, and the Shoulder of Mutton inn, around a small green. **Meadle** is another hamlet in the same parish, beside the Lower Icknield way, with a large cruck barn at Wooster's Farm.

IVER

Map p.143, D1
4 miles E of Slough on the B470

A glance at the map, suggests that the building of the nearby M25 must have been disastrous for Iver. In fact, by relieving the place of a huge volume of unwanted traffic, the M25 has helped to preserve some authentic village atmosphere in what is now quite a large community. Iver is at its best in the area around the green fringed by the timber-framed Swan Inn, the church and the bridge over the Colne.

⛪ St Peter's Church has a Saxon nave, and much of its castellated tower dates from the 13th century. Inside, there are some striking monuments. The most unusual depicts a shrouded woman rising from a black coffin. Two of the other memorials are dedicated to sailors. One was a midshipman killed in battle; the other, an 18th-century admiral, survived to reach retirement in his Iver garden, where he specialized in growing pansies.

🏛 Bridgefoot House to the north-east of the church is a fine, early Georgian building of yellow and red brick. Yellow brick was also used for **Iver Lodge**, an elegant early 19th-century house north of the church. A little way along from there is **Coppins**, formerly the home of the Duke and Duchess of Kent. The best house in the village, however, is **Iver Grove** in Wood Lane at its junction with the Langley road. This baroque mansion, built in 1722, shows the great influence of Christopher Wren.

South of Iver across the canal is **Richings Park**, where **Pope's Walk** recalls the poet Alexander Pope's pleasure in the area.

IVER HEATH

Map p.143, C1
4 miles NE of Slough on the A412

Iver Heath has expanded since Victorian times into a large village around crossroads branching to Slough, Uxbridge and Denham. It has an essentially suburban air, softened by parts of the original heathland by which it was surrounded. The area had few residents before then, although the heath already had a network of tracks used by people passing through, and those who preyed upon them: the infamous 18th-century highwayman Dick Turpin was said to have taken more than a passing interest in the heath's travellers.

The village church is St Margaret's on the Denham road. It was built in 1862 when the number of homes in the area was rapidly increasing. The Tudor-look Warren House to the west of the church dates from 1881.

The 1930s brought glamour to the area with the development of Pinewood film studios. Their situation near pine trees at the north-west corner of the village was one reason for the name. The other was to suggest that Pinewood, with a huge sound stage that was then the biggest in the world, would come to rival Hollywood. But although many famous films, including the James Bond series, have been made in the Pinewood studios, Hollywood remains unchallenged. It is hard to believe that many Iver Heath residents, who clearly enjoy their peacable existence, are seriously disappointed.

IVINGHOE

Map p.150, E4
7 miles E of Aylesbury on the B489

It is said that Sir Walter Scott adapted the name of this village for the title of his novel *Ivanhoe*. Whatever the truth, it is certain that Ivinghoe was once far bigger and more flourishing than it is today. Situated at the junction of the Roman Lower and Upper Icknield Ways, its streets are lined with handsome 17th- and 18th-century buildings, including a court house (now the Parish Room) and a former town hall.

Old buildings are also clustered near the 17th-century King's Head Hotel opposite the church. Ivinghoe is close to the eastern end of the Ridgeway path, and a youth hostel in the village attracts walkers either starting or finishing their trek across the Chilterns to or from Avebury in Wiltshire.

St Mary's Church is an enormous building, dating back to the 13th century. Restored by the church-builder G.E.Street in 1871, it contains a number of intricate interior details. The grotesque corbels on the roof posts are carved with biblical characters and angels, and the Jacobean oak pulpit portrays a carved figure of Jesus stepping from the tomb.

The ends of the pews are decorated with carved poppy heads and various 15th-century figures, including one of a mermaid. Brasses in the church commemorate Richard Blackhead (d. 1517) and his wife, and members of the Duncombe family. Outside, hanging on the church's boundary wall, is an 18-ft hook once used to tear thatch from blazing buildings to prevent fire from spreading. Below it is an awesome iron man-trap built to catch poachers.

Ford End Watermill, in Station Road, is 18th-century, as the initials of miller

William Heley and the date 1795 on the wall show. Restored by the Pitstone Local History Society, it uses an overshot wheel driven by water from the stream behind. Demonstrations of grinding are regularly given throughout the summer, on Sundays and Bank Holidays.

The Ridgeway starts two miles out of the village, at **Ivinghoe Beacon**, which commands superb views from its 800-ft summit, and which formed part of the chain of beacons lit across England to warn of the approach of the Spanish Armada in 1588. From here, visitors can see right across the Vale of Aylesbury and the Ashridge estate, which together with the Beacon Hill, were given to the National Trust in the 1920s. The remains of an Iron Age fort and a barrow thought to be Bronze Age can be seen on the hill.

Ford End Watermill: 0296 668223.

JORDANS

Map p.142, A3
3 miles E of Beaconsfield off the A40

The village of Jordans is a recent creation, having been built in the early part of this century by the Society of Friends – the Quakers – who still own it. But it has a long history, with roots stretching back to the early 17th century when William Penn (see PENN) and other Quaker notables held meetings at William Russell's farmhouse, now called 'Old Jordans'. For many years such meetings were unlawful, but with the passing of the Toleration Act in 1688 the Quakers spread their wings, and The Friend's Meeting House was built near the farmhouse. Old Jordans was not forgotten, however, and it is now run by the Society as a 40-bed guest house and conference centre. In its grounds is the Mayflower Barn, constructed about 1630 of timber from the *Mayflower*, the ship that carried the Pilgrim Fathers to New England in 1620.

When 102 acres of nearby land came up for sale, the Quaker community formed a consortium to buy the land themselves, in order to protect the character of their environment. And so it was that building of Jordans commenced in 1919, with Frederick Rowntree, of the famous Quaker confectionary family, as architect. It was completed in 1923, and a 'self-governing human community' (as the consortium described it), in line with the Friends' social and religious principles, came into being. Modest houses, let on monthly tenancies, were built around a substantial village green, with a co-operative shop and post office and, of course, no pub.

Management of the village was vested in a 12-member committee, comprising representatives of the shareholders, the Society of Friends, and the tenants themselves. Jordans is still run along similar lines today and, as its founders hoped, retains much of its unique character. The small village has its own seat on CHALFONT ST GILES Parish Council.

William Penn and a number of his contemporaries – including Thomas Ellwood, who brought John Milton to Chalfont St Giles – are buried at Jordans, which has become a focal point for Quakers from all over the world.

KINGSEY

Map p.145, B1
1 mile S of Haddenham on the A4129

The name of the village originated from 'The King's Eye', situated as it was on an 'island' in the low-lying water meadows to the south of HADDENHAM. It is close to the border with Oxfordshire, defined here by the Cuttle Brook, and has been in both counties during its history. It is a small village, no more than a few scattered cottages and the 19th-century church of St Nicholas.

🏠 The late 17th-century **Tythorp House** is set in parkland that extends from the west of the village to the county boundary. The house is not open to the public and its plain, rendered appearance gives no indication of the splendid interior with its grand staircase and Rococo plasterwork from the 18th century.

The hamlet of **Aston Sandford** is isolated down a narrow lane, a mile north west of Kingsey. There are a few brick and stone cottages, opposite a low, brick wall and tiled roof that hide the grounds of the Rectory. There is a red brick manor beside the churchyard. The tiny St Michael's Church has a nave and chancel built of limestone and a restored timber bellcote.

LANE END

Map p.141, A1
4 miles NW of Marlow on the B482

A large village that has grown to the size of a small market town, Lane End is a discordant mix of old cottages, Victorian brick terraces and modern infill. Like many settlements in the High Wycombe area, it was once a chair-making centre. But the old workshops are now converted to other uses, and a spread of new development – small industrial, council and private housing estates – has arisen to the north, held in check by the M40. Symptomatic of this mutation is the fact that Lane End's most prominent building is now a car repair garage occupying a triangle in the central crossroads, opposite a small pond and a plain Wesleyan chapel of 1835.

Approached from the B482, it is not immediately obvious that that the village is built around two separate, large commons.

The north common is overlooked by the Chairmakers Arms pub, part of a terrace of gabled flint cottages whose walls are patterned with diamonds of red brick. There is a small group of red brick and knapped flint cottages in the middle, next to a stream, surrounded by a white picket fence. On the south side, past a row of modernized Victorian cottages beside a small green, is another rough common on three sides of the churchyard.

⛪ **Holy Trinity Church** was built in 1878 of knapped flint and Bath stone, with a tower that was given extra height in 1901. Its most venerable feature is the 14th-century roof timbers, which come from an old barn at Bisham Abbey in Berkshire.

Past the church a lane continues to Moor Common, with a late 17th-century flint and brick farmhouse entered through an arched, brick gateway.

The hamlet of **Wheeler End** is half a mile to the north. Its houses are widely spaced around a large common on either side of a steep wooded valley which, before it was separated by the M40, connected with the commons at Lane End.

LATHBURY

Map P.154, B2
1 mile N of Newport Pagnell on the B526

The only tangible evidence on the B526 of Lathbury's existence – apart from the village name signs at the roadside – is a large, red-brick, Georgian manor, fronting directly onto the western side of the road, which is now a residential home for the elderly. The remainder of this tiny settlement, a scattering of old and new houses set beside the Ouse, is along a narrow street leading off the B526 immediately to the north of the Manor House.

All Saints' Church, at the far end of the village, is another of the square-towered churches so favoured in this part of the county. Although it is claimed to date back as far as the 9th century, the structure is basically medieval, with a 13th-century tower and some 12th-century details in the interior, most of which was rebuilt in the 14th century.

LATIMER

Map p.147, D2
3 miles SE of Chesham off the A404

Tucked discreetly away in the Chiltern Hills above the water meadows of the Chess valley, abutting the Hertfordshire border, is the little village of Latimer. It is a picturesque collection of mid-Victorian, leaded-window cottages, grouped around a modest triangular green on which stand a canopied water pump and a pink stone obelisk commemorating villagers who perished in the Boer War.

The village has close historical connections with the Cavendish family, later to become the Barons Chesham, who lived in nearby Latimer House. And nowhere are these links better exemplified than in the green's third feature: a stone cairn erected, rather eccentrically, to the memory of a horse.

The third Baron Chesham, a major general and Knight Commander of the Order of the Bath, commanded British troops in the Boer War, his main adversary being General Count de Villebois Mareuil, a one-time commander of the French Foreign Legion. The two men had a warrior's respect for each other, and when de Villebois was killed and his horse injured at the Battle of Boshof, Lord Chesham had the animal transported to Latimer, where it lived a further 11 years in peaceful retirement. On the death of the horse – 'Villebois', as it had been renamed – its heart and ceremonial trappings were reverently interred on the village green.

Latimer House, set to the west of the village in an elevated position above the Chess, was once the seat of the Cavendish family. Originally an Elizabethan manor house, it was gutted by fire in the 1830s and faithfully reconstructed by the first Baron Chesham. Visited regularly by Victorian prime ministers Gladstone and Disraeli, it is now a conference centre owned by accountants Coopers and Lybrand. The House is surrounded by extensive parklands – Latimer Park – at the village edge of which is the small, parish church of St Mary Magdelene, built by the first Baron at the time of the rebuilding of Latimer House.

LAVENDON

Map p.156, E4
2 miles NE of Olney on the A428

Astride the busy Bedford to Northampton road lies the fairly large village of Lavendon

– the northernmost in the county. At its centre, adjacent to one of the two sharp bends in the main road, is a stone cross war memorial, behind which, on raised ground, dominant and prominent, stands the church of St Michael.

With its cream-coloured stone and imposing square tower, **St Michael's Church** is similar in style and character to many other village churches in the north of Buckinghamshire, although it is older than most, dating back in parts to Saxon times. The church grounds lost 9 ft of their frontage in the 1950s to accommodate improvements to the A428, which still seems wholly inadequate for the heavy and constant flow of traffic it carries through this village. Sadly, by-passes seem to have passed Lavendon by.

LECKHAMPSTEAD

Map p.153, E1
3 miles NE of Buckingham off the A422

The Leck stream, a tributary of the nearby Great Ouse, runs through the little valley where the village nestles, and gives it its name. There is no real village centre: Leckhampstead's houses are scattered in four almost separate groups.

The Bishop of Bayeaux, the commissioner of the famous tapestry, was a principal landowner in the area after the Norman conquest. Remains from the Norman era can still be seen in Leckhampstead's 12th-century Church of the Assumption, near the stream, which has some fine Norman doorways.

At one time, a pub stood close to the church, to the irritation of one 19th-century incumbent, the Reverend Heneage Drummond. A man of some means as well as of decision, he bought the pub and promptly closed it down. Drummond was rector in Leckhampstead for almost 50 years, and clearly left his mark: there is still no pub in the village; nor even a shop.

The narrow Limes End Bridge crossing

the Leck was restored in 1993, and off the main road there is a car park which makes a useful starting point for riverside walks.

THE LEE

Map p.146, C3
2 miles N of Great Missenden off the A413

For drivers unfamiliar with The Lee, approaching at night from the south-west can be a startling experience. For as you enter the village around a slight bend, your headlights pick out a huge, ruddy-faced head peering at you over a tall hedge. This apparition is actually a two-ton, solid oak bust of Admiral Lord Howe, and was the figure-head on the eponymous Victorian warship (later re-named HMS Impregnable), the very last wooden man-of-war to be built for the Royal Navy.

The bust stands in the grounds of a private house called 'Pipers', and was placed there in 1921 by Captain Ivor Stewart-Liberty after the ship had been de-commissioned and its timber bought by the Liberty family for use in the mock-Tudor extension of their famous store in London's Regent St. The store's founder was Sir Arthur Liberty, a second-generation haberdasher from CHESHAM who became Lord of the Manor of The Lee and whose descendants still live at 'Pipers' today.

The Lee lies within a sparsely-populated and densely-wooded part of the Chiltern Hills, rising nearby to 790 ft above sea level, the highest point within the Chiltern District. At its heart lies a conservation area, comprising a triangular village green around which are cottages and a pub of flint and brick.

The **Church of St John the Baptist** is on the north-west of the village about 200 yds from the green. The red-brick structure was built in 1867, extended soon afterwards by the addition of a chancel, funded by the Liberty family. A footpath leads through the peaceful churchyard to what is now called 'The

Hambleden

87

Old Church', built in the 12th century of chalk and clay, and totally hidden from view from the road. The east window of the old building depicts the images of 17th-century 'champions of liberty', including Lord Protector Oliver Cromwell and John Hampden.

LILLINGSTONE LOVELL

Map p.152, D4
5 miles N of Buckingham off the A413

Lillingstone Lovell is one of Buckinghamshire's most northern villages, barely a mile from the Northamptonshire border; it is also one of the county's most unspoilt. Just two miles south-east of the Silverstone motor-racing circuit, its status as a conservation area has restricted the number of new homes; it is still largely an agricultural community, consisting mainly of farmhouses set back on driveways from the main road. The village was originally known as Lillingestane before it was purchased by the baronial Lovell family in the early 15th century.

The Church of the Assumption has a tower and porch arch built in 1210, with aisles added in the 14th century and much restoration in the 19th. Inside are fine brasses and ornaments.

Lillingstone Dayrell, less than a mile to the west, is a tiny village on the Buckingham to Towcester main road, easy to skip past almost without noticing. There are only a few cottages and a pub at the roadside, with the village church in parkland nearby.

Lillingstone Dayrell's Norman **St Nicholas's Church** retains its original walls, tower and chancel arch. Inside are some fine tiles, 14th-century or older, and the grand tomb of Paul Dayrell, who died in 1571. He was a descendant of the Dayrell family who gave the hamlet its name. He lies in armour alongside his wife Dorothy, while the small figures of the couple's many children kneel around their parents' tomb.

LITTLE HAMPDEN

Map p.146, C2
3 miles NW of Great Missenden on minor roads off the A413

A tiny village set on a steep, wooded hillside in a remote part of the Chilterns, Little Hampden comprises a small church, some attractive old cottages, the Rising Sun pub, tucked away at the end of a narrow lane, and the white-rendered Manor Farm, opposite the church.

The village forms the hub of a network of woodland paths and is a popular stop for walkers. There are good walks to Whiteleaf Cross (see WHITELEAF) in the west and north to COOMBE HILL, the highest point in the Chilterns. There are other walks, south to GREAT HAMPDEN, and east to THE LEE, crossing the main railway line to AYLESBURY by the bridge at Mayortorne Manor.

Little Hampden Church (it has no known dedication) has a 13th-century chancel and, inside, wall-paintings from the same period, depicting a row of standing figures – but, alas, they are incomplete thanks to a rebuilding programme of 1859. Externally, its most prominent feature is a timber-framed 15th-century porch, whose upper storey does duty as a belfry.

LITTLE ICKFORD

Map p.144, B3 ★
3 miles SW of Long Crendon off the A418

Although now linked to Ickford by modern buildings at the east end of the village, the small hamlet of Little Ickford still retains its own identity. There is a short lane, lined with long, half-timbered cottages, some of which are thatched. The lane ends at a group of stone cottages beside a rambling, white-painted, stone and timber-framed house. At the start of the lane there is a chequered brick house, a half-timbered cottage and a pond overhung with willows. New Manor House, opposite the pond, is a timber-framed, cream-coloured house with a twin-gabled roof, large wings and tall gabled porch. The adjoining farm buildings are thatched and weatherboarded. There is a footpath from the hamlet to SHABBINGTON.

LITTLE KIMBLE

Map p.146, B1
2 miles NE of Princes Risborough on the A4010

A small village, straddling the Upper and Lower Icknield Way, Little Kimble is divided in two by a noisy main road. It has its own British Rail station on a branch line to Aylesbury, but its real distinction is its church.

All Saints Church** is surrounded by clipped yew trees and has a mainly 13th-century exterior of knapped flint with stone buttresses. It was restored in 1876 – at which time a bellcot and north porch were added – but it has survived the experience well. The simple, unspoilt interior is renowned for its early 14th-century wall paintings of which several large segments remain, including St George and the Princess, St Francis preaching to the birds, and a Last Judgement. The church also has a plain, Norman tub font, some 13th-century floor tiles and a 17th-century panelled pulpit.

LITTLE MARLOW

Map p.141, B3   ★
2 miles NE of Marlow off the A4155

With its large, triangular green, church and manor house, this pretty village is a quiet backwater beside the busy road from Bourne End to MARLOW. The green, now a cricket pitch, is connected to the church by a short street lined with red brick and flint cottages. From the church, at the bottom end of the street, a path leads to the towpath on the north bank of the River Thames. The King's Head pub is at the other end, opposite the green, while the second pub in the village,

appropriately called The Queen's Head, is in Pound Lane, next to the timber-framed Saltings House. The large, walled garden belonging to the 17th-century Manor House occupies land between Pound Lane and the churchyard. The timber-framed house has an 18th-century front and a long, gabled roofline. There is a brick dovecote in the walled garden. Manor Farm, a timber-framed, gabled house, is at the bottom of the street, beside the church lich-gate.

St John the Baptist's Church stands in a damp churchyard on the edge of a stream and marshy woodland. It is built of rough rendered flint and clunch, a soft, chalk stone, commonly used in the Chilterns. The 12th-century nave has 14th-century side aisles which give the church a distinctive, triple-gabled roof, whose dormer windows are a replica of the 17th-century originals. The sturdy, flint tower is also 14th-century, while the irregular shape of the church is further enhanced by the twin-gabled chancel that is offset from the nave.

Well End is an attractive group of flint and brick cottages a mile to the east of Little Marlow. Abbey Farm incorporates some 13th-century remains from the Benedictine nunnery that occupied the water meadows beside the river.

LONG CRENDON

Map p.144, B4   ★★
3 miles W of Haddenham on the B4011

A large village set on a hill above the River Thame, Long Crendon has one of the area's finest collections of old buildings, dating from the 15th century onwards. Its size and arrangment gives it something of the appearance of a market town: there is a small square, a long street leading up to the church and an imposing manor house. It was important for needle-making, which flourished from the 16th century until 1830, when industrialization elsewhere made handcraft-based production uncompetitive.

89

The Square, surrounded by a mixture of brick and stone houses, with some more recent additions, is in the south west corner. In Frogmore Lane, past rows of stone and thatched cottages, at the top of a steep hill, is the 15th-century **Long Crendon Manor**. The house, built in stone and partly timber-framed, with a gabled, stone porch and massive stone wings including a high gatehouse, forms three sides of a courtyard that is open to gardens on the west. The Hall and east wing are contemporary with the original house, but the timber-framed west wing was added in the 16th century. The picturesque appearance of the house owes much to improvements made in the 1920s.

The High St, which starts on the other side of the Square, must be one of the best preserved streets in the county. It winds between rows of stone, brick, timber-framed and thatched cottages from the square to Church Green, where a cluster of cottages step down a grassy lane beside the churchyard. **Madges** is a long, half-timbered, partly brick and thatched house with a double height carriageway and weatherboarded farm buildings in a yard at the rear. The symmetrical, late 17th-century, stone Manor House, beside the church, is on the site of an older manor.

⛪ St Mary's Church★ is built of grey stone with a large, central tower, an unusually broad, short nave with wide side aisles, transepts and a chancel. It is mostly 13th-century, although the north aisle and transept were altered in the 14th century. Later alterations, notably the south and west porch and the upper part of the tower, were made in the late 15th and 16th centuries. The spacious interior includes a decorative timber roof over the chancel, which has a large, 19th-century window, a copy of that in the north transept. There is a painted monument to Sir John Dormer (d.1626) behind a 17th-century screen in the south transept. The octagonal font is 14th-century. There is a fine view from the churchyard towards the Chiltern Hills.

▥ The 14th-century **Court House★** is a long, jettied, timber-framed building beside the church gate. It was probably built as a wool store or staple hall, as the village wealth in the medieval period was derived mainly from the wool trade. The whole upper floor was originally one long room, with an open queen post roof, and a smaller adjoining room. It was later used as a court house, from the reign of Henry V, and remained so until the late 19th century. It was one of the first buildings to be acquired by the National Trust, in 1900. The upper floor is open to the public.

Lower End is an attractive row of stone and thatched cottages, including the Angel Inn and the thatched Chandos Arms, along a swath of green beside the Bicester Road. It was once a separate 'end' of Long Crendon (see HADDENHAM), but is now joined to the village by a mixture of Edwardian and more recent buildings.

A footpath from Long Crendon churchyard leads a mile eastward to the ruined **Notley Abbey** on the River Thame. The original abbey, which rivalled that of MISSENDEN for importance, was a 12th-century monastic Augustinian foundation; after the Dissolution, the present private house – also Notley Abbey – was converted from the 14th- and 15th-century Abbot's Lodging, incorporating the Hall, the Parlour, Solar and part of the cloister. Of the rest of the Abbey, only some of the foundations survive, with the south-east corner from the 12th- and 13th-century nave and chancel, and the circular pier bases at the crossing, above which once stood the rebuilt 15th-century tower.
Long Crendon Court House: Apr–Sept: Wed 2–6pm; Sat, Sun & BH Mon 11am–6pm.

LOWER WINCHENDON

Map p.149, F1
1 mile N of Cuddington on minor roads

The village, which sits amid the water meadows of the River Thame, is made up

of a church, a mansion – Nether Winchendon House (see p.21) – and a few cottages and farm houses scattered around a central green. Also known as Nether Winchendon, the village was listed in the Domesday Book as a possession of Notley Abbey (see LONG CRENDON), but was given to the first Earl of Bedford after the Dissolution in 1547. Today, the ochre wash that colours numerous witchert and timber-framed houses indicates they belong to the Spencer-Bernard family, the ancestral owners of Winchendon House.

There is an unusual Victorian post box on the village green, set into a circular stone column with a stone ball on top.

⛪ St Nicholas's Church, just off the green where the three lanes in and out of the village meet, features an unusual single-handed clock, brought from Winchendon House in 1722 and eventually restored in 1967. Its enormous pendulum, which reaches to the bottom of the bell tower, can be seen inside. The church has a Jacobean pulpit, dated 1613, a timber gallery bearing the Royal Arms (of George II) and a row of high box pews. The windows feature 15th-century glass in the south aisle and 16th-century Flemish glass to the south of the church.

LUDGERSHALL

Map p.148, E3
5 miles W of Waddesden off the A41

An out-of-the-way village laid out in a loose square at the Western end of Aylesbury Vale, Ludgershall has become even more out of the way since the disappearance of the railway station that once connected it with the rest of the surrounding countryside. A mixture of old and new, the village's houses are scattered around the ancient church in the centre.

⛪ The 14th-century **St Mary's Church** is a limestone rubble building with stone dressings and a low lead roof. The south aisle contains the tomb of George Grenville, Prime Minister between 1763

and 1765. A tomb chest with brasses commemorates Anne English, who died in 1565, and her daughter and granddaughter. John Wycliffe, the heretical religious reformer, once held the living of Ludgershall, but was never a resident.

MAIDS MORETON

Map p.152, E4
1 mile NE of Buckingham on the A413

Maids Moreton stands on high ground overlooking Buckingham. Modern development has intertwined with old, grey stone houses and well-maintained cottages.

⛪ Dominating the village, the 15th-century limestone **St Edmund's Church** stands to the south of the main Moreton Rd. It was founded in 1450 by two daughters of the rich land-owning Peover family – the 'Maids' of the village's name. Interesting features include the elaborate fan-vaults and a fading 16th-century wall painting of the Last Supper.

Maids Moreton is today almost a suburb of Buckingham, but in former times the villagers had their own way of doing things. Until the war and the start of rationing, a Main St baker fired his oven every Sunday morning to cook joints for villagers. Husbands would take home the roasts after a customary pre-lunch pint at the pub. In the 1930s, the most notable local character was 'Captain Starlight', who returned from soldiering in World War I and dug himself a pit to live in. He stayed there, stargazing every night, until his death many years later.

MARLOW

Map p.141, B3   ★★
4 miles S of High Wycombe on the A404

The town is one of the best preserved of its size in the county, with the added charm of a riverside setting (picture, p.91). It grew up around Market Square on high ground above the River Thames, where the Henley road, passing along West St, met the road from Reading to High Wycombe, now the High St. A stone obelisk in Market Square, which displays the distance in miles to Oxford and London, was erected in 1822. The old Town Hall, built in 1807 by Samuel Wyatt, faces the High St. It is now the Crown Hotel, but during the Napoleonic War, among its less willing guests were French prisoners of war.

The road from Henley meets the town at Western House, at the still rural end of the fine **West St**★. The chequered brick house, set back behind a wall with a brick summer house on the corner, was built in 1699. Further on is **Ramnatz**, a large 18th-century house with an adjoining stable block. It was used, like many of the larger houses in the town, by the Royal Military College, which came to Marlow from High Wycombe in 1799 and stayed until 1811, when it moved to its present home at Sandhurst.

On the north side of the street stands a long terrace of knapped flint and red brick buildings, the Sir William Borlase Grammar School, founded in 1624. The adjoining row of Gothic-style cottages is now also used by the school. In one of them, **Albion House**, Mary Shelley wrote her novel *Frankenstein* in 1818. West St continues towards Market Square in an almost unbroken line of 17th- and 18th-century houses, which includes by far the most cohesive group of Georgian buildings in the town. The continuation of the London road into Spittal St is less interesting, except for Borlase Cottages, a long terrace built in 1788 at its eastern end, in Chapel St.

The **High St**★ rivals West St for its selection of fine buildings, and between them they best represent the Georgian character of the town. The old Post Office has an imposing brick façade, with a pediment, heavy timber cornice and a fluted, Ionic doorcase. The Brewery offices of Thomas Wethered & Sons (now owned by Whitbread) have a tall, red brick façade on one side of the yard and a white painted, stuccoed façade, with semi-

circular bays, on the other. At the lower end of the street there are two more fine examples of 18th-century houses. Brampton House is built of red brick with a parapet, rubbed brick cornice and fluted doorcase. The End House has a hipped, mansard roof, a tall bay on its end gable and a Doric porch.

The most striking feature of the river is the town's elegant suspension bridge, built in 1831–6 by W. T. Clark, from which the view upstream is over water meadows on the Buckinghamshire side. A larger copy of the bridge was subsequently built across the Danube at Budapest.

The 19th-century **All Saints' Church**, by C. F. Inwood, stands beside the bridge, with its churchyard on the river bank opposite Marlow Weir. The tall nave and smaller chancel are built of pale brick, but the tower is of knapped flint with stone quoining and has a slender, stone spire, added in 1899. The interior has several monuments retained from the older church, including one to Sir Miles Hobart (d.1636), depicting his death in a coach accident in Holborn. The marble and stone pulpit is by G.E.Street.

There is a small green beside the church, lined by the houses in the Causeway. These include the red brick, gabled Vicarage, built in 1865 by Street, and the 18th-century George and Dragon. There is a path beside the church to the slipway at the bottom of St Peter St, where the roar of the weir is always in the background. There is a pleasant row of cottages with semi-circular, Dutch gables in chequered brick, which includes The Two Brewers pub. The grandest building in Marlow faces the top end of the street. **Marlow Place** was built for John Wallop in 1720 by Thomas Archer.

It is a large, symmetrical, brick-built house with a pediment supported on giant pilasters of rubbed, red brick. The **Old Parsonage** is opposite, in St Peter St. It is a rambling mixture of materials from different periods, including brick, stone and timber framing, with a 14th-century hall and an attractive roofline of steep, tiled

gables. The Deanery, a chequered brick house, is joined to it on the south side.

🏛 **St Peter's Church**, set back from the street behind a tall, copper beech hedge, is of knapped flint with a tower and broach-spire. It was built in 1848 by Pugin, but the proportions of the small church have been irrevocably altered by the addition of a modern chapel at the chancel end.

The path at the bottom of the street continues downstream, between high brick walls, until it reaches Marlow Lock. The lock is below the weir, between the north bank and Lock Island, from where there are pleasant views of Marlow Bridge and All Saints' Church. Further downstream, Mill St joins the towpath to Bourne End.

Perhaps the best known ceremony to be connected with this stretch of the river is 'Swan-Upping', in which all the swans between Blackfriars, in the City of London, and Henley-on-Thames are collected and marked. The other principal event on the river is the Marlow Amateur Regatta, which is held on one day in June, in the run-up to the more famous Henley Regatta.

MARSH GIBBON

Map p.148, C2
4 miles E of Bicester off the A41

Marsh Gibbon lies by the River Ray close to the Oxfordshire border. The village is a densely-packed maze of little streets, in which are intertwined houses of different eras and materials, including brick and tile, thatch, and rendered brickwork. There is a 16th-century manor house near the 13th-century St Mary's church.

The village is also the home of the Greyhound Club, not a dog-racing association but one of the country's oldest friendly societies, founded in 1788 by a group of bellringers and named after the pub where they held their meetings.

Friendly societies were the predecessors of modern insurance companies; their members contributed to a mutual fund that paid out on death or illness. The Marsh Gibbon Greyhound Club is still going strong after more than 200 years. So is the Greyhound Inn, which is still the village pub.

The hamlet of **Twyford**, two miles north-east, has enjoyed total tranquillity since the old main rail line that passed close by was dismantled. Its **Church of the Assumption** has a wealth of Norman features and a splendid 15th-century porch.

MARSWORTH

Map p.150, E4
1½ miles SW of Ivinghoe on the B489

Canals criss-cross Marsworth, which is built on the junction of the Grand Union Canal and its Aylesbury arm. The village has several canal-side pubs, including the timber-framed Red Lion in the old village centre. The village is also on the edge of Tring reservoir, a nature reserve just over the Hertfordshire border.

Once part of the estate of Lord Rosebery of Mentmore Towers (see p.19), Marsworth had its own hospital in the 19th century. This was demolished in 1894 and Hospital Farm now stands on the site. During the Second World War, Cheddington airfield just north of the village was a USAAF bomber base. The site is now an industrial estate, but the airfield's perimeter fence and some of the original buildings survive. There is a memorial on the roadside to airmen from the base who lost their lives.

🏛 **All Saints' Church** in Church Lane in the old part of Marsworth is a 14th-century building constructed of flint and clunch. The north side of the church was widened in the 15th century and further restorations were carried out in 1828 and 1854. The

The Point Entertainment Centre, Milton Keynes

pulpit is set on a 14th-century capital. Church monuments include a brass to one N. West, who died in 1586, and a splendid 16th-century tomb chest that is apparently the work of Epiphanius Evesham, one of the earliest English sculptors to leave his name as well as his work.

MEDMENHAM

Map p.141, C1
4 miles SW of Marlow on the A4155

This comfortable village is set back from the Thames on a lane that runs down to the old ferry, now lined with Victorian houses in large gardens. There are some smaller cottages of flint or timber framed with brick infill in the lane and another, stone and timber-framed group beside the Marlow road. They shelter beneath a chalk cliff, all that remains of a small quarry. Across a stream, below the church, the gables and jettied, ivy-clad upper floor of the 15th-century Manor House can be seen behind a topiary hedge.

On the wooded slopes above the village is Lodge Farm, a 17th-century vignette of gabled, timber-framed farm buildings that dominates the hillside. From the bottom of Ferry Lane a riverside path runs upstream to MILL END.

🛏 Near the river, **St Peter's Church** is built in a mixture of chalk and flint, with a white rendered, castellated tower. The church has two Norman doorways and a 15th-century tower. It has a plain interior, with nave and chancel combined under a single roof, and a small north transept.

🏛 **Medmenham Abbey** (a house, not an abbey) stands on the site of a real Cistercian abbey founded in the early 13th century; but the oldest part of the present structure dates back only to the 16th century and most of it is the result of 19th-century rebuilding. The house became briefly notorious in the 18th century when the libertine Chancellor of the Exchequer Sir Francis Dashwood used it as a venue for the fancy-dress orgies held by his Hell-Fire Club, whose

members were otherwise known as 'The Mad Monks of Medmenham' (see also WEST WYCOMBE).

MENTMORE

Map p.150, D3
3 miles NW of Ivinghoe off the B488

Mentmore village, a collection of cottages and mock-Tudor houses along an elm-lined green, is dominated by Mentmore Towers (see p.19) the immense Rothschild country house built by Sir Joseph Paxton in 1855. When Baron Meyer de Rothschild moved to his new family seat, the village was much rebuilt in a fashion that reflected the his passions for hunting and horses.

In the estate's heyday, nearly everyone who lived in the area was employed on it – in the stables, the kennels, the gardens and grounds (at one time, 44 gardeners were employed), or in the house itself. Besides establishing a stud at the nearby hamlet of Crafton, the Baron built a hostel in Ledburn (a mile to the north of the village) to house his stable lads and trainers. This has become the Hare and Hounds Inn, where visitors can see a few memorabilia of the Great Train Robbery of 1963. (See CHEDDINGTON).

A small 15th-century brick-built manor house is hidden in trees on the east side of the park attached to Mentmore Towers.

🛏 **St Mary's Church**, on the north-east side of the park, is built at the highest point of the village. Restored in 1858 by G.H.Stokes, the son-in-law of Sir Joseph Paxton, the church is of late Norman origins. It is constructed of orange ironstone with grey stone dressings, and the inside is whitewashed in the 19th-century style.

One of the monuments is to Neil James Primrose, younger brother of the Lord Rosebery who had inherited the Towers. Primrose was killed leading the last British army cavalry charge, made by the Royal Buckinghamshire Hussars at El Mughar in Palestine in November, 1917; one of his Rothschild cousins died in the same action.

MILTON KEYNES

Map p.154, D2
Immediately W of the M1 (Junctions 13 and 14)

Conceived in the late 1960s and still being developed today – with a population of 185,000 and a target of 250,000 by the end of the century – Milton Keynes is Britain's newest city, based around and now incorporating the three established towns of BLETCHLEY to the south and STONY STRATFORD and WOLVERTON to the north-west. Eighteen villages and smaller settlements have also been digested, some dating back to medieval and Norman times or before. One of them, MILTON KEYNES VILLAGE, gave its name to the new metropolis.

Although commonly referred to as a city, an appellation encouraged by its Development Corporation, in civic and local government terms Milton Keynes is designated only a borough. Created by the Local Government Act 1972, and coming formally into existence in April 1974, the Milton Keynes Borough Council includes not only the immediate conurbation of Milton Keynes itself, but also the various nearby parishes and former urban and rural districts of north Buckinghamshire up to the Bedfordshire and Northamptonshire borders, including WOBURN SANDS, NEWPORT PAGNELL and OLNEY.

The commercial and civic heart of the new city, known simply as **Central Milton Keynes**, is an impressively clean, environmentally-attractive area that was planned and built on a green-field site between older villages. Smart buildings, many with reflective glass exteriors (picture, p.94) and all low-rise, with about five stories as the maximum, are set well back from tree-lined boulevards, leaving a general impression of space and lack of clutter.

The main indoor shopping arcade in Central Milton Keynes is to the east of Saxon Gate between Silbury Boulevard and Midsummer Boulevard, parallel streets running east to west. One of the largest

indoor shopping centres in Europe, it accommodates over 130 shops, restaurants and bars, and a garden centre.

Outside of Central Milton Keynes, the main arterial roads throughout the conurbation have been constructed (and the course of pre-existing roads altered) to create a grid system that runs broadly east-west ('horizontally') and north-south ('vertically'). Each road, in addition to its name, is given a letter and number, from V1 to V11 and H1 to H10.

The system, with every road clearly identified at each of the many roundabout intersections, is of great help to visitors and probably to many residents too. Roads within the individual grid squares give access to the various suburbs, villages, trading estates and communal amenities that make up this extraordinary city. Central Milton Keynes itself, for example, is bounded by V5 to the west, V8 to the east, and H5 and H6 to the north and south.

Although Central Milton Keynes includes an identifiable commercial sector, the planners have quite deliberately spread the centres of commercial and industrial activity throughout the city, minimizing commuter congestion and enabling many people to to walk to work.

Like the new housing development, the various small industrial and commercial estates and retail parks are well-landscaped, with trees now coming to maturity, often to the extent of being hidden from the view of anyone driving along the arterial grid roads. And the new city's 'lungs' are not limited to roadside tree planting. The city is studded with woods, lakes and recreational parks, some very large, some carefully landscaped, others left more naturally as wildlife habitats.

🌷 **Elfield Park,** for example, with access from Watling St (V4) south of Chaffron St (H7), contains the Milton Keynes Bowl, an open air concert arena, while in Campbell Park – to the east of Central Milton Keynes, entered via Portway (H5) or Childs Way (H6) – there is an open air theatre, a summer venue for opera, plays and folk music. Most of the parks also contain some of the modern statues and sculptures that are a feature of Milton Keynes.

Ⓜ Robert Koenig's carved oak column sculpture, 'Metropolis', and Ray Smith's steel 'Chain Reaction' are both in Campbell Park, and Newlands Park – off Brickhill St (V10) north of Childs Way (H6) – is home to an unusual sculpture by tree-planting, 'Tree Cathedral'. Liz Leyh's controversial 'Concrete Cows', which many who have never visited Milton Keynes sneeringly assume to sum the place up, are in North Loughton Valley Park to the north of Monks Way (H3), where they can be seen from the road. Other modern sculptures are found around the shopping arcade and the civic offices in Central Milton Keynes.

The large-scale earth-moving required to build Milton Keynes made it the most intensively studied archaeological landscape in Britain, and many discoveries, ranging from small artefacts to entire ancient settlements, are exhibited throughout the new city.

For example, the discovery in 1967 of some fragments of pottery led to the unearthing of a Roman villa and nearby farm buildings at Bancroft. The site is within North Loughton Valley Park, just 200 yds or so from the 'Concrete Cows'. In the same park, south of Monks Way, are the remains of Bradwell Abbey, a 12th-century Benedictine Priory.

🏛 East of Great Monks St (V5), and approached by Gloucester Road and Southern Way, is the **Milton Keynes Museum of Industry and Rural Life** (unusually in this city, run by a private trust and not by the Borough Council) housing a collection of artefacts and memorabilia of agriculture, transport and local industry.
Milton Keynes Museum: Easter– end Oct, 1.30–4.30pm. Tel: 0908 316222.
Milton Keynes Tourist Information Office: 0908 232525.

MILTON KEYNES VILLAGE

Map p.154, D3
2 miles W of Central Milton Keynes on the A4146

The planners of MILTON KEYNES have been careful to retain the tranquil atmosphere of the medieval villages that are now part of this modern conurbation. Thus there are only two vehicular routes into Milton Keynes Village, from Tongwell St and Chaffron Way (respectively V11 and H8 on the Milton Keynes grid system), although there is further access by footpath, cycle-track and bridleway.

At the centre of the village, prominently at the junction of Broughton Road and Willen Road, is a white-painted, thatched, public house, the Swan Inn, attractively adorned outside with well-tended and colourful flower-tubs and hanging baskets.

⛪ Along Willen Road, opposite the village hall, is the ancient church of All Saints, a particularly well-maintained example of the medieval, square-towered, cream-coloured, stone churches so abundant in the old villages of north Buckinghamshire.

MONKS RISBOROUGH

Map p.145, C3
1 mile N of Princes Risborough off the A4010

Once owned in Saxon times by the monastery at Canterbury (hence its name), Monks Risborough has gradually been absorbed by the adjacent market town of PRINCES RISBOROUGH, which has steadily encroached across the fields that formerly separated the two settlements. Now all that is left of a distinctive Monks Risborough identity is a row of half-timbered, thatched cottages clustered around a church, lapped closely by its expanding neighbour.

⛪ **St Dunstan's Church**, with a flint tower and square stair turret, was restored by G.E. Street in 1864, but much remains

of its earlier glories. There is a fluted Norman font, an arcade of 14th-century otagonal piers, and a late 15th-century rood screen with nine painted panels depicting the Apostles. The church also contains some fine 14th- and 15th-century stained glass, and there are splendid brasses set among the medieval tiles on the floor.

MURSLEY

Map p.149, A3
3 miles E of Winslow off the B4032

Mursley is halfway between Buckingham and Dunstable and was once a bustling market town. Today, it is something of a backwater, mostly serving Milton Keynes as a commuter dormitory. But mingled with post-war council housing, there are still some substantial brick houses and a few thatched cottages.

In its heyday, it enjoyed considerable wealth, largely due to Sir John Fortescue, a cousin to Queen Elizabeth I and former Chancellor of the Exchequer. In 1570, he acquired the manor of **Salden**, then a hamlet close by, where he built a mansion at a cost of £33,000 The completed estate included terraced gardens, a bowling green, a lake and its own windmill to grind corn. It attracted a royal visit from Elizabeth; James I followed on an occasion in 1603 when 22 gentlemen were knighted. Today the remains of the mansion are part of a farm, one mile east of Mursley down the narrow Cooks Lane, opposite the village church.

The painstakingly restored 14th-century **St Mary's Church**, off Main St in Mursley, is almost a shrine to the Fortescue family, with many fine memorials to Sir John and his kin. The church has a Jacobean pulpit.

NASH

Map p.153, F3
5 miles E of Buckingham off the A421

A small village in the heart of the Whaddon Chase hunting territory, Nash has a number of old cottages, some thatched, spread around village lanes and All Saints' Church, built in 1958 in pale brown stone on the little High St. There is an almost classic village pond (recently regenerated by local children, who won an ecology award for their efforts) with a wooden bridge; in the summer, the scene frequently attracts artists, who set up their easels on the green.

There are several good springs in the area, and the ease of obtaining clean water probably attracted the first community to settle here. Today, it is mostly occupied by commuters, who are more interested in the peace and quiet it still offers.

NEWPORT PAGNELL

Map p.154, C2
3 miles NE of Milton Keynes, off the M1 (Junction 14)

Regular drivers on the M1 will know Newport Pagnell best for its service station. However, away from the motorway lies a town of medieval origin, (picture, p.99) which takes its name from the Pagnell family, one-time owners of the land. At the time of the Civil War, it was an important garrison town for Parliament. A young John Bunyan served there under the town's governor, Sir Samuel Luke, as did one Captain Oliver Cromwell (son of Lord Protector) who contracted smallpox and died there in 1644. Today it is probably more interesting for its industrial heritage than its architecture; among its manufacturers is Aston Martin Lagonda, producers of exotic sports cars.

Newport Pagnell is bisected both by the B526 and the River Ouzel (also known as the River Lovat), a tributary of the Great Ouse, which it joins just to the east of the town. Road and river meet at a cast iron bridge that was erected in 1810, the oldest in England still in daily use for traffic. The journey of the cast sections from the foundry in Rotherham was by sea to London, by canal to GREAT LINFORD, and then the last few painful miles by cart to Newport Pagnell.

⛪ The **Church of St Peter and St Paul**, to the right of the B526, heading north-west, and in a raised position overlooking the River Ouzel to the rear, is a large example of the medieval, square-towered, cream-coloured stone churches much in evidence in surrounding villages. The tower is Tudor, and the fine interior has a 15th-century roof.

NEWTON BLOSSOMVILLE

Map p.156, E4
2 miles E of Olney off the A428

The small village of Newton Blossomville gets its name from the Blossomville family, owners of the land during the 13th century, rather than from any inherent prettiness. None the less, attractive stone cottages, thatched roofs and hanging baskets make the village worthy of its name. With the exception of some local authority housing on the western edge, newer buildings have been constructed to blend in well.

⚥ The name of the village pub catches the eye: **The Old Mill That Burned Down.** It was indeed an old mill, and it became a pub – called, quite reasonably, The Old Mill. However, the building was gutted by fire in the 1980s and re-opened under its present unusual, if factually-accurate, name. Iconoclasts will be cheered by the fact that its carved oak bar was once a cathedral pulpit.

⛪ The **Church of St Nicholas** stands at the eastern end of the village, where the main street double-bends its way towards the Bedfordshire border. Fourteenth-century in origin, it was restored in 1862, but still retains some of its original stained glass. Its past incumbents include William Warburton, literary executor to the poet Alexander Pope and later to become Bishop of Gloucester, who was rector here in the 1720s.

A public bridleway at the side of the church leads to a series of five bridges over a large area of reed banks, where the Great Ouse divides temporarily into several channels.

NEWTON LONGVILLE

Map p.154, D2
5 miles S of Central Milton Keynes off the B4034

Newton Longville has been a brickmaking village for centuries, and is still easily distinguished by the great brickworks chimneys that dominate its skyline. Perhaps surprisingly, many of its own neat houses are mainly timber-framed or stone, often with thatch, and it has a pleasantly medieval appearance.

However, neither its appearance nor its prosperity may endure, for the London Brick Company closed the works in 1990, and the village faces an uncertain future. Plans to use the old industrial site for new housing estates will probably lead to Newton Longville's absorption by nearby BLETCHLEY.

⛪ **St Faith's Church** is of Norman origin, with a massive, 15th-century tower. The interior is noted for its fine stone carving, of which there are examplesdating from the 12th century right up to modern times.To the south of the church is the early Elizabethan manor house.

NORTH CRAWLEY

Map p.154, C4
3 miles E of Newport Pagnell

North Crawley is the starting point for several of the country walks promoted by Milton Keynes Borough Council, ranging from four to six miles. The leaflet detailing them is number five in the series Countryside Walks published by the council, obtainable from various local libraries or the Tourist Information Office in MILTON KEYNES. It is a well-established little town that seems to have changed little over the decades.

⛪ The 11th-century **Church of St Firmin**, on the south side of High St, set back from the road, is one of only two churches in England dedicated to this obscure 3rd-century saint, the first bishop

of Amiens, who was martyred in the year 287. The inhabitants of Little Crawley, a hamlet just to the north-west, strongly opposed attempts in the 16th century to annexe them to the neighbouring parish of Chicheley, firmly declaring their allegiance to St Firmin's, where they had paid their tithes, contributed to the restoration of the church wall, and had long buried their dead.The church has one 13th-century arcade, and carved 15th-century roofs.

Crawley Grange, in the north-east of the village, can be approached by footpath, but walkers should bear in mind that the Grange and its grounds are private property. The most famous resident of this Tudor-style manor house was Cardinal Wolsey, but it passed into private hands after King Henry VIII confiscated church property. Henry's daughter, Elizabeth I, stayed here in 1575, and the interior is said to display her coat of arms. Sadly, the house is no longer a single unit, but has been converted into four separate residences.

NORTHEND

Map P.145, F1
3 miles SW of Stokenchurch on minor roads

Northend is a large hamlet of 16th- and 17th-century flint, red brick or rendered cottages dotted around a triangular green, open to fields on one side, with a large pond, overhung by trees, at one end. There is a pub, the White Hart, at the opposite end of the green, and a village hall, the former schoolroom and schoolhouse.

Beyond the pond, a track leads to Wormley Park, passing Northend Farm, a handsome 17th-century house refronted in the 18th-century with a symmetrical flint-and-brick façade and a central canopied door. The back has a steep, sweeping plain tiled roof and the outbuildings include the original weather-boarded barns and a restored granary, which was moved away from the house and rebuilt after being blown down in a storm.

The best approach is from TURVILLE, along a sunken lane through woodland with superb views over the steep sided Turville Valley towards the Wormsley Estate (see IBSTONE). Northend, along with SOUTHEND, is really an 'end' of Turville, two miles to the east, neither having its own church. It is not unusual for larger villages to consist of a collection of 'ends', as at LONG CRENDON or HADDENHAM, but here they are further from Turville than FINGEST, the next village in the valley.

NORTH MARSTON

Map p.149, C2
2 miles NW of Whitchurch off the A413

A small village on a hill overlooking open pastures, North Marston was in medieval times a popular place of pilgrimage. A great fire destroyed much of the old village in 1705, but there are still a number of half-timbered and thatched cottages along the High St.

The pilgrims' goal was the village church – or rather, its rector John Shorne (or Schorne) and his miraculous spring. Shorne came to the parish from Monks Risborough in the south of Aylesbury Vale in 1290 and established a name as a miracle worker and healer during his 24-year residence. The chalybeate spring (now protected by a wooden cover) in the village was said to have bubbled up when Shorne struck the ground with his stick. Claimed to be the source of Shorne's healing powers, the waters were reputed to be a cure for eye infections. Whatever miraculous properties the spring might have possessed, its bacteriological purity may have saved the villagers of North Marston from infection during a cholera epidemic which claimed many lives in the area in 1835.

Shorne's most famous achievement was to confine the devil himself in a boot – a tale represented in countless inn signs and stained glass windows the length of Britain.

Buckinghamshire Railway Centre, Quainton

The story is also said to have inspired the Jack-in-the-box toy. After Shorne's death, pilgrims travelled for miles to see his tomb, until in 1478 the jealous Dean of Windsor obtained permission from the Pope to have the rector's remains re-interred in St George's Chapel there.

St Mary's Church itself has a 13th-century tower, north aisle and arcade, while its south aisle dates from the 14th and 15th centuries. The roof has brackets carved with angels playing musical instruments, and the choir stalls are carved with poppy heads and misericords. The chancel is Perpendicular, with a two-storey vestry and priest's room. There is a monument to John Virgin (a rector of the church who died in 1694) with a painted hand pointing to the floor and the inscription: 'He lise just down thare.' Richard Saunders, physician to Queen Elizabeth I is commemorated in a brass dated 1602.

Another royal connection was established by Queen Victoria who, in 1855, paid for the church's restoration as a gesture of thanks for a legacy made by the London solicitor John Camden Nield. Nield, who had a well-earned reputation as a miser, owned a great deal of property in Buckinghamshire, including land in North Marston. Perhaps to infuriate his kinsfolk (in which ambition he certainly succeeded) he bequeathed his whole fortune, the staggering sum of £250,000, to the Queen 'for her sole use and benefit'. The will held up in court, and a delighted Victoria promptly purchased the Balmoral estate.

OAKLEY

Map p.148, F2
4 miles N of Long Crendon, on the B4011

Mentioned in the Domesday Book as Achelia (and later known as Ockley), the village of Oakley lies in water meadows at the foot of Brill Hill, on the edge of the vestiges of Bernewoode Forest, a former royal hunting ground. The village houses are of all ages and types. Two worth more than a glance are the brick-and-stone

Oakley House, built in 1660 and distinguished by its stone mullion windows, and the Georgian rectory which adjoins the church.

The village is surrounded by farms, one of which briefly made Oakley the centre of world attention in 1963. Leatherslade Farm was chosen as a hideout by the Great Train Robbers because the surrounding trees hid the house from the road. The gang occupied the farm on and off for three months before carrying out their sensational crime at CHEDDINGTON on 8 August. Much of the evidence which secured their subsequent convictions was found here – such as Ronnie Biggs' fingerprints on a Monopoly board the gang played with to pass the time. Visitors to the now partly-demolished farm are not encouraged.

St Mary's Church has seen many alterations since it was first built in the 12th century. The latest of these is an incongruous concrete and wood porch added in 1960. Inside, the north arcade is lined with circular and octagonal columns, and the north aisle contains a 14th-century coffin lid decorated with crosses.

OLNEY

Map p.154, A3
5 miles N of Newport Pagnell on the A509

Although unremarkable at first sight, this modest market town carries a substantial accumulation of tradition and cultural history. It sits astride the A509 (which forms Olney's High St) between Milton Keynes and Newport Pagnell to the south and the Northamptonshire towns of Wellingborough and Kettering in the north. From whichever direction Olney is approached, the spire of the parish church, rising 180 ft out of the valley of the Great Ouse, dominates the view (picture, p.107).

The small, triangular Market Place, abutting the eastern side of the A509, is still clearly the town centre. On its southern side stands **Orchard Side**, an imposing red-brick house where from 1768 to 1786 the poet William Cowper lived. It was while living here that Cowper wrote his most famous poem, the comic ballad *The Diverting History of John Gilpin*. Orchard Side now houses the Cowper and Newton Museum, dedicated jointly to the poet and to the Reverend John Newton, the slave-trader turned preacher who so influenced him. Both were important hymn-writers, together publishing the Olney Hymns in 1799. Cowper's hymns included *God Moves in a Mysterious Way*; Newton wrote *Amazing Grace*, as well as *How Sweet the Name of Jesus Sounds*. The museum contains many personal belongings, including paintings, portraits, books and manuscripts.

On a somewhat less exalted plane, the famous Olney Pancake Race dates originally from the 15th century. After many interruptions, it has now been run on every Shrove Tuesday since its resurrection in 1948. The 415-yd race starts promptly at 12 noon outside The Bell public house on the western side of Market Place. The winner receives the 'kiss of peace' from the vicar, after which competitors, officials, townsfolk and visitors pack the church for the Shriving Service and sing several of Cowper's and Newton's Olney Hymns.

The High St is mainly to the north of the Market Place, and includes a selection of interesting antique shops and a factory making lace – once an important industry in Olney and nearby villages. On the western side of High St, north of the Market Place, runs a quarter-mile terrace of properties (shops, houses, and offices), mainly Victorian in appearance, but seemingly built at different times and to different designs.

At the very southern end of the town, the A509 bridge over the River Great Ouse, though altered and modernized to accommodate modern traffic, dates originally from the 18th century. From the bridge, nearby Emberton Country Park (see p. 25) is clearly visible close by to the south west; conversely, the best view of the bridge's original stonework can be had from the park.

🕍 The **Church of St Peter and St Paul**, once in the charge of John Newton, stands on the banks of the Great Ouse at the southern end of the town, east of High St. Like many nearby village churches, it is in the Decorated style but its great spire makes it unusual in the county. Newton's grave was transferred here from London in 1893, and there is a window dedicated to the memory of Cowper.
Cowper and Newton Museum: *Apr–Oct 10am–12 and 2–5pm; Nov–March 2–4pm. Tel: 0234 711516.*

OVING

Map p.149, D3
1 mile W of Whitchurch off the A418

Set on a limestone crest, the village (pronounced 'Ooving' by locals) commands a breathtaking view across the Vale of AYLESBURY to the Chilterns, with Aylesbury's concrete County Hall protruding in the middle. Oving consists of a few cottages and farmhouses in a little square of roads around the church. The 17th-century timber-framed Black Boy pub is opposite the church and its back garden has another splendid view – this time northward to the CLAYDONS and NORTH MARSTON.

🏛 Also in the village are an 18th-century brick and stone rectory and **Oving House**, an early 17th-century building that was once the home of Charles Pilsworth, an MP for Aylesbury. Oving spreads south west to the hamlet of **Pitchcott**, which has a farmhouse and a few cottages and St Giles's Church, a small grey stone building with a 12th-century nave that was over-restored in 1864.

🕍 Oving's **All Saints' Church** contains the fragments of a 15th-century painting of Christ depicted with the tools of his trade – a warning against the evils of working on a Sunday. As well as a 13th-century nave and chancel there is a plain 15th-century tower and an aisle chapel added in the early 14th century; the south aisle has 15th-century carved bench ends in the south aisle. The church, like so many others in the area, was restored by G.E.Street in the 19th century.

PADBURY

Map p.149, A1
4 miles NW of Winslow on the A413

Padbury has a range of interesting homes, from 16th-century cottages to Edwardian villas. The village is now split by the busy A413 Buckingham–Aylesbury road; its old central thoroughfare, Main St, slopes gently south-west away from the church and the traffic-laden road. The area behind the old school has a number of thatched and half-timbered cottages. To the south-west is the River Lovett, where there are traces of an ancient earthwork known as **Norbury Camp**.

⌂ The 13th-century **St Matthew's Church** has a 15th-century tower with 18th-century chimney-pot toppings. The interior includes rare, but fading, 14th-century wall paintings depicting the life of St Catherine.

PENN

Map p.146, F4
3 miles E of High Wycombe on the B474

The word 'penn' is Celtic for 'wooded hill'; hence the name of this village, high on the wooded Chiltern Hills. The land rises 200 ft in the short distance from Beaconsfield, and it is said that, when conditions are right, 12 counties can be seen from the top of the church tower. Within the village, there is much green space and common land, and although its architecture is relatively indistinguished, it remains unscarred by new development.

Penn shares its name with its most famous son: William Penn (1644–1718), non-conformist, Quaker, and founder of the state of Pennsylvania. Repeatedly imprisoned for his beliefs – after one bout of seditious publishing he ended up in the Tower of London – he eventually sailed to America and claimed territory granted to his father, Admiral Sir William Penn. There he established a home for his co-religionists, governing, it is said, wisely and with tolerance. He returned to England to campaign on behalf of those still imprisoned on account of their religious beliefs, as a result of which, in 1686, over 1,200 Quakers and other non-conformists were released. After spending more time in America, where he managed to mitigate a little the evils of slavery, he returned finally to England in 1701. He died in 1718 and is buried in the nearby Quaker settlement of JORDANS.

The village later produced a somewhat less admirable character in one Jack Shrimpton. Born around 1750, the son of Penn's church warden, Shrimpton became a notorious highwayman working the commons around GERRARDS CROSS. He was eventually caught in Bristol and hanged for murder.

⌂ The 11th-century, flint **Church of the Holy Trinity**, on Church Road, houses the Penn family vault, in which are buried five of William Penn's grandchildren. There are also the vaults of family of the earls Howe, whose family home, Penn House, is between Penn and nearby PENN STREET.

The road out of Penn towards BEACONSFIELD to the south-west is lined with expensive-looking properties, and exudes an air of genteel affluence. On the left of the road is The Crown pub, extensively covered with Virginia creeper, a saturated flame-red on bright, autumn days, and with a beautiful, eye-catching Chilterns scene as a backdrop.

PENN STREET

Map p.146, E4
3 miles NE of High Wycombe off the A404

Penn Street is the name of a tiny hamlet best known for being the location of Penn

Olney

House and for its unusual, mid-19th-century church. Lanes leading to the village are abundant with wild rhododendrons, giving a delight of colour in late May and early June. It has an expansive village green, complete with a stone obelisk war memorial.

🏠 **Penn House**, to the south of Penn Street, is home to Lord and Lady Howe – not the Tory politician, but the seventh Earl Howe and Viscount Curzon. The earldom was bestowed in 1821 upon Richard Howe, a naval officer who rose to become first Lord of the Admiralty, and whose likeness in the form of a two-ton, solid oak bust – once the figure-head on the Royal Navy's last wooden warship – is now sited in the nearby village of THE LEE.

⛪ **Holy Trinity Church** lies to the north of the green and is approached through the gates to the Rectory. Designed in 1849 by Benjamin Ferrey, biographer of the English Gothic architect Augustus Pugin, it is unusual in these parts in that it has a spire: and no ordinary spire, at that. It is octagonal (atop an octagonal tower) and is constructed of oak shingle. On either side stretches the main body of the church, built of the familiar local flint with stone dressings.

PITSTONE

Map p.150, E4
1 m S of Ivinghoe off the B489

The old and new parts of Pitstone village are separated into two distinctly different areas. **Church End**, containing the isolated church on the edge of open Chiltern fields was the extent of the place until earlier this century. When the Tunnel Cement Company came in the 1940s Pitstone expanded to take in the estate of red brick houses that forms **Pitstone Green**. Mining here is an age-old tradition – there are Neolithic flint mines in a one of the nearby Chiltern scarp slopes – but now the cement factory that worked the gigantic chalk and clay pits is winding down and the future of the site is uncertain. But the

Pitstone Local History Society has made sure the village is an extremely interesting place to visit.

🏛 **Pitstone Green Farm Museum** has been used by the Pitstone Local History Society for many years to display old farm machinery. The farm has been in the hands of the Hawkins family since 1808 and the current owner is intent on using it to show several hundred years of farming traditions. There are exhibitions of the implements used in lacemaking (once a strong Buckinghamshire industry) and straw-plaiting (backbone of the hat industry previously centred at nearby Luton). A farmhouse kitchen has been permanently set up in one room and others feature crafts tools once used by carpenters, cobblers and plumbers.

A recent addition to the museum is a 1914 Crossley gas engine once used to power machinery at Grace's mill in Tring. It started life providing power for the Picture Palace at Kingston-upon-Thames.

Pitstone Windmill is said to be the oldest surviving post mill in the country. Situated just off the B488 before IVINGHOE, its silhouette from the road forms an incongruous picture with the giant towers of the cement works behind it. Its timbers show dates of 1627 and 1749, but it was badly damaged in a storm in 1902. The windmill was given to the National Trust in 1937, who restored it with the help of the Pitstone Local History Society in 1963. Now volunteer members of the village's windmill committee open it to visitors on Sundays and Bank Holidays throughout the summer.

⛪ **Pitstone Church**, (formerly St Mary's) on a hill in the Church End part of the village, is very much out of place in modern Pitstone. Now redundant and disused, it is kept alive by volunteers from the Pitstone Local History Society who open it, like the windmill, to summer visitors. With mainly Perpendicular architecture, it displays an unusual layout: the chancel and tower are off the centre line of the nave. There is a 17th-century Jacobean pulpit, an 18th-century communion rail and a brass dating back to the 1500s showing a lady in early 14th-century dress. There is a painting dated 1733 above the chancel arch depicting the Royal Arms, the Commandments, the Creed and the Lord's Prayer. The nearby parsonage was built in 1856 by the church architect G.E. Street.

Pitstone Church: *Summer season, Sun and BH, varying hours. Tel: Mr Morris, 0296 661544*
Pitstone Windmill: *The National Trust (Tel: 0494 528051) or the Windmill Committee (Tel: 0296 668227).*
Pitstone Farm Museum: *Summer season, last Sun in month and BH Mons; also special activity days. Tel: 0296 668223 or 0296 661997.*

PRESTON BISSETT

Map p.148, A3
3 miles NW of Steeple Claydon on minor roads

Preston Bissett is a quiet backwater of a place, a good base for country walks close to the Oxfordshire border, especially through the Tingewick and Lenborough woods less than a mile to the north.

⛪ The **Church of St John the Baptist**, at the centre of three village lanes, has an engagingly stumpy 15th-century tower and high windows to the nave. Much of the rest is 14th-century, and there are some curious carvings on the outside walls, iincluding a monkey and a jester. There are fine archways inside.

⚲ Across the churchyard are the **White Hart** and **Old Hat** pubs; the latter has been run for years as an old-fashioned domestic sitting room with a bar. Unlike its appearance, its prices are not pre-war.

PRESTWOOD

Map p.146, D2
1 mile W of Great Missenden on the A4128

Noted in days gone by for its extensive cherry orchards, Prestwood has now grown to the size of a small town, almost merging with its near neighbour, GREAT MISSENDEN;

and in so doing, it has lost much of the character which doubtless it once had.

It was certainly favoured by the immediate post-war prime minister, Clement Attlee, who, having come to love the Chilterns countryside when staying at his official country residence at Chequers, bought Cherry Cottage in Prestwood when he left office in 1951. When he was elevated to the peerage in 1955 as Earl Attlee, he took the secondary title of Viscount Prestwood.

PRINCES RISBOROUGH

Map p.146, C1   ★
7 miles NE of High Wycombe on the A4010

This market town, originally called Great Risborough, occupies a gap in the Chiltern Hills on a main railway line to London and at the meeting point of several roads. Its once compact medieval core is now encircled by residential estates that have grown steadily from the 1930s onwards. The High St is lined with 18th-century houses, many of which have been spoilt by modern shop fronts. The triangular Market Square surrounds a tiny Market Hall, built in 1824. It has a small clock turret and an open, timber colonnade around its base. In Church St there are half-timbered, gabled houses leading from the square, but these soon give way to modern buildings.

The town has recently acquired an unusual monument to a narrow escape. Outside the Public Library where High St meets Bell St, the tailfin of a B-17 Flying Fortress bomber cast in bronze commemorates the 1943 sacrifice of Lt Clyde Cosper USAAF, who stayed with his stricken, bomb-laden aircraft and brought it down clear of the town at the cost of his own life. The young pilot's heroism was recognized only in 1992.

⛪ **St Mary's Church**, in a shaded churchyard close to the Market Hall, is built of knapped flint with stone quoining. It has a chequered patterned tower with a stone spire. The spire was added in 1908 by John Oldrid Scott, but the appearance

of the remainder of the 13th- and 14th-century church owes much to the alterations by Arthur Blomfield in 1868. There is a panelled, Jacobean pulpit which survived the Victorian restoration, together with the triple lancet window in the south aisle.

The 15th-century, timber-framed Vicarage is in the lane beside the church.

Manor House*, facing the church across a tree-lined lane, is a 17th-century, red-brick house. It has a symmetrical front with five bays, tall sash windows and decorative brick pilasters. There is a fine Jacobean oak staircase inside, with strapwork balustrades cut out of the solid wood. The panelled drawing room, with its heavily moulded chimney piece, is 17th-century, but the house was probably remodelled from an earlier house. It is now in the ownership of the National Trust and may be visited by arrangement with the tenant.

Manor House: Wed 2.30–4.30pm; garden by appointment, weekends Apr–Sept. Tel: 0494 520941.

QUAINTON

Map p.149, D1
6 miles NW of Aylesbury off the A41

An H-shaped village dominated by a disused windmill, Quainton is in a position (at more than 500 ft above sea level) to survey the whole of Buckinghamshire north of the Chilterns. The village green, which forms the cross-bar of the H, is the site of the Quainton Cross. Reputedly dating from the 14th century, the stone block and shaft was once used as a meeting place for preachers and as the assembly point for funeral processions on their way to the church at the east end of the green.

Cross Farmhouse, a chequered brick building with a carved stone panel bearing the date 1723, is nearby, built by Justice Dormer for one of his daughters. There is also a 16th-century rectory, fronted with 18th-century red brick nearby. **Denham**

Lodge, once the manor house of the Winwood family, surrounded by a moat and approached through a single-storey gatehouse, is to the north east of the village.

The **Winwood Almshouses**, dated 1687, are of dark brick and feature Dutch gables and large chimneys. Quainton's Magpie Cottage was the home of George Lipscomb, author of the *History of Antiquities of the County of Buckingham*, who died penniless in a debtor's prison in 1846. The Buckinghamshire Railway Centre is to the south of the village at the old Quainton Road railway station (see p.27; picture, p.102).

Quainton Windmill, standing about 90 ft high, was built of local brick around 1830. Unused since the 1880s, it was restored in 1976. The mill is the last of three which once worked in the village.

The **Church of St Mary and The Holy Cross** is noted for its impressive monuments. A stone building with tiled roofs, it is mostly 14th- and 15th-century. The chancel was rebuilt and the church restored by William White in 1877. Inside are an octagonal font and a late 15th-century painted screen showing four saints. The most impressive of the monuments is that of Robert Dormer, Justice to the court of Common Pleas who died in 1726. In a large tomb attributed to the French sculptor François Roubillac, the judge is shown next to his wife making a sorrowful gesture to his son, who died just a few months before him and is portrayed lying on the stone sarcophagus.

Richard Winwood, who founded the village's almshouses, is shown life-size in plate armour, with his wife. Margery, wife of Sir Ralph Verney, is depicted in another memorial dated 1685 as the daughter of John Inwardby ('Lorde of this towne') and is shown alongside her children. There is also a grey and white marble sarcophagus signed by Giacomo Leoni containing the remains of one Sir Richard Piggott. The many brasses in the church date between 1350 and the 17th century.

Three Locks, Soulbury

QUARRENDON

Map p.149, E3
1 mile NW of Aylesbury off the A41

A few hundred yards along the footpath that leads off the A41 just north of Aylesbury is the site of Quarrendon, a vanished medieval village of which little remains but its name on the map. Lying amid the water meadows of the nearby River Thame, Quarrendon was once the site of the Lee family mansion, by all accounts a large house surrounded by a moat, the traces of which remain. Sir Henry Lee, an ancestor of the American confederate General Robert E.Lee, entertained Queen Elizabeth I to dinner there in 1592. His monument stood in the 13th-century St Peter's Church, a few yards away. But now only but a few fragments of that building remain.

Elsewhere in the vanished village are signs of trenches and other earthworks dug during the Civil War. Quarrendon was of strategic importance for Parliament forces defending Aylesbury against Prince Rupert's army and the Battle of Holman's Bridge in 1642 was fought nearby; the dead from that exchange now lie in HARDWICK church. St Osyth, the 7th-century Christian martyr, was born at Quarrendon.

RADNAGE

Map p.145, E3
2 miles NE of Stokenchurch on minor roads off the A40

The village, a small cluster of 16th-century cottages, 18th-century rectory and a church, is just one of several hamlets that make up the 'ends' of Radnage (see HADDENHAM). These scattered groups of cottages are variously known as Radnage Bottom, Town End, Church End, Radnage Common, Bennett End, Sprig's Alley and – curiously – The City, but none is as pleasant as Radnage itself.

Footpaths connect the various 'ends', several leading up to Bledlow Ridge, north of the village, from where there are good views across the valley towards BRADENHAM in the east and the Vale of Aylesbury to the north. From Rout's Green, on the other side of the ridge, there are paths connecting with the Upper Icknield Way above BLEDLOW, two miles to the north.

The village of **Bledlow Ridge**, on the topographical feature of the same name, is a ribbon of mainly 1920–1950 red brick and rendered houses and bungalows, architecturally uninteresting but sheltering very comfortably in large gardens. More recent structures line the steep hill on the opposite side of the ridge from Radnage.

⌂ St Mary's Church★, Radnage, sits in a deep fold in the Chiltern Hills, backed by beech woods, with splendid views from the churchyard over the village and countryside beyond. Built of rough rendered flint with stone quoining, its early 13th-century nave and chancel are separated by a central tower of the same period. The nave was extended, its roof raised, and a south porch added in the 15th century, but the simple interior still bears the outline of 13th-century wall paintings on the north and east walls.

RAVENSTONE

Map p.156, F1
3 miles W of Olney off the B526

A challenger to its near neighbour WESTON UNDERWOOD, a mile or so to the east, for the title of Buckinghamshire's Best Kept Village, Ravenstone is a delight. The cream-coloured local stone – the material used to build most of the old cottages (and newer properties, too) – is easy on the eye, and the residents clearly take much care with their thatches and gardens and great pride in the whole appearance of their village.

The main street winds gently uphill towards the north-east where, hidden away on the left hand side, is the Church of All Saints, with a monument to Heneage Finch, first Earl of Nottingham and King Charles II's Lord Chancellor.

SEER GREEN

Map p.147, F1
2 miles SW of Chalfont St Giles off the A355

The origin of the name of Seer Green is based firmly in legend, for it was said to be the resting place of Merlin, King Arthur's 'seer', on his journeys to and from Camelot, when local inhabitants would come to consult him about their futures and fortunes. The village grew to share a tradition of liberalism and Quaker nonconformity with the adjacent community of JORDANS, and also became known colloquially as 'Cherry Pie Village' on account of its once-extensive cherry orchards that supplied markets in London.

Today, Seer Green, and its approach road from BEACONSFIELD to the south-west, has become comfortable but expensive commuter territory, with its own British Rail station tucked discreetly out of sight along Farm Lane.

SHABBINGTON

Map p.144, B3
2 miles SW of Long Crendon off the A418

Standing on the Oxfordshire border by the River Thame, Shabbington is a small village of red-brick houses, thatched cottages and farmhouses, peppered about with modern development. The large, stone built Hill House stands beside the church; the School House is 17th-century with an 18th-century front and large Gothic window.

⛪ St Mary Magdalene Church is a mixture of all ages. The main body was built in the 11th century, the chancel windows date from the 13th and the squat, stone tower was added in the 1600s. The Victorians, meanwhile left their mark in the form of new nave windows and a north porch.

The church is attractively situated in a low-lying position by the river, but subsidence has clearly been a serious problem. Its tower lurches against huge buttresses, and the rough stone interior provides an alarming perspective, with outward leaning walls, a cambered floor and a chancel arch that is narrower at the bottom than the top. For the present, the building still seems solid; but further subsidence could cause a collapse. There is a curious, shuttered window in the north wall of the chancel and an early 17th-century pulpit. A stone cross in the churchyard commemorates the dead of both the World Wars.

SHALSTONE

Map p.152, E2
4 miles NW of Buckingham off the A422

Shalstone is a secluded village of thatched stone cottages between Stowe (see p.21) in Buckinghamshire and Brackley just across the Northamptonshire border. Its **Church of St Edward the Confessor** looks Victorian thanks to major restoration in the last century; parts of it are actually 15th-century.

A tree-lined drive opposite the church leads to the private Georgian dwelling **Shalstone House**, which is built on the site of the village's old manor house.

SHERINGTON

Map p.154, B3
2 miles NE of Newport Pagnell off the A509

A substantial but unremarkable village, Sherington now serves mainly as a commuter and dormitory settlement for nearby Milton Keynes and Newport Pagnell.

⛪ Its greatest interest is its Church of St Laud, curiously the only one in all England dedicated to the saint (a French bishop of the 6th century) The church is a fine example of the Decorated style. Begun in the 13th century, it has a central tower begun in that period and is built of the familiar, cream-coloured local stone. The interior is particularly bright, with a glowing clerestory and a fine west window.

SLAPTON

Map p.150, D4
3 miles N of Ivinghoe off the A4146

A small village on the Bedfordshire border, Slapton has the River Ouzel on one side and the Grand Union Canal on the other. The hamlets of **Horton** and **Horton Wharf** on the canal form part of the parish. There are fine views looking towards the Chilterns and Dunstable Downs.

Slapton is mostly composed of modern housing. Nevertheless, there are village stories of ghosts that wander the streets at night, including a well-known old lady dressed in black crossing a long-vanished footpath, and a young girl who chases a runaway horse.

The **Church of the Holy Cross** is a chalky limestone building with origins that go back to 1223. The chancel was rebuilt in the 19th century when a lead roof was also added. Inside there are several brasses from the 15th and 16th centuries.

SOULBURY

Map p.150, B3
2 miles E of Stewkley on the B4032

The hilltop village of Soulbury is one of several in the area that escaped destruction when the government turned down the Roskill Report's recommendation to site a third London airport here in the 1970s: a great relief to inhabitants and visitors alike, for it is a pleasant old place.

In the centre of the village is a large block of Derbyshire Millstone Grit. Technically, the stone is a glacial erratic: that is, a piece of debris picked up by a glacier in its drift south, then deposited when the ice melted. However, local myth has imbued this particular stone with magical powers and there are tall village stories of its moving, unassisted by human hand, at certain times of the year.

Liscombe Park, a mile to the south, was the country mansion of the Lovett family for nearly 600 years. Set in grounds behind gates on the Leighton Buzzard road, the house is a red-brick mansion built originally in the 16th century but much altered. since. The Lovetts are recalled in the parish church and at Lovetts School (dated 1724), now a private house, opposite. Soulbury's other mansion, **Chelmscote Manor**, is on the main A4146 road, half a mile south of Three Locks. Also a private house, it encompasses a 14th-century chapel.

Three Locks, one mile north-east of Soulbury on the main road to Bletchley, sits on the Grand Union Canal. The locks were built in 1800 and later improved to raise boats nearly 20 ft as they begin their ascent into the Chilterns. The date of each lock is shown in the stone at the side of each. The pub alongside contains beams from the stables that once completed this canalside stopping point (picture, p.110).

All Saints' Church is on the top of the hill in Soulbury. Inside, the earliest of the monuments to the Lovett family of Liscombe Park is to Robert Lovett, dated 1491. The memorial to Sir Robert and Lady Lovett (both 17th-century) is topped with kneeling figures in armour and black robes. Another Robert Lovett, this time a former sheriff of the county, is commemorated in a white marble sarcophagus decorated with cherubs, with an urn on top. The tomb (dated 1699) was made by Grinling Gibbons. The church is built of rendered ironstone and has a 12th-century nave and chancel which was rebuilt in the 14th century.

SOUTHEND

Map p.140, A4
7 miles NW of Marlow on minor roads off the B480

In this part of the world all 'ends' lead to TURVILLE. NORTHEND is one, Southend is

Waddesdon Manor, Waddesdon

another. It comprises a cluster of 16th- and 17th-century flint and brick cottages grouped around a small common with extensive views towards Turville, a mile to the north, to which it is linked more directly by footpath than by the narrow lanes threading their way through the wooded valleys.

Turville Heath is a scattered group of houses around a common, mid way between Northend and Southend. Two of them are especially fine. To the west is Turville Park, an early 18th-century classical, stuccoed house built for William Perry. Turville Grange is also 18th-century, built of red and grey brick, and surrounded by picturesque farm buildings one of which boasts a weatherboarded tower.

The road from the nearby hamlet of **Summer Heath** winds through a broad valley towards FINGEST with distant views of the steep, wooded slopes of Great Wood, passing another attractive group of farm buildings at **Dolesdean** until, eventually, the Turville windmill comes into sight.

STEWKLEY

Map p.150, B2
8 miles N of Aylesbury on the B4032

Often described as the longest village in England, Stewkley runs for nearly two miles along its main road – a mile on either side of its church, with new and old buildings, including several timber-framed farmhouses from the 16th century, scattered at irregular intervals. In the days when Stewkley was a thriving centre with six grocers, ten pubs and a healthy straw-plaiting industry, the northern 'uptown' and 'downtown' were almost two separate communities, but the village is quieter and more unified now.

Recorded in the Domesday book as 'Steuchlai', it has a church that is regarded as one of the finest intact Norman buildings in Britain. But village, church and all would have disappeared beneath advancing bulldozers had the government accepted a 1970s plan to transform the whole area into a third London airport. Fortunately, local protesters defeated the

project, and Stewkley still stands.

These were not the first protestors in Stewkley's recent history; the feminist activist Sylvia Pankhurst, daughter of the suffragette Emmeline, lived in a house in Stewkley's Ivy Lane between 1912 and 1914.

The **Church of St Michael and All Angels**, stands surrounded by yews in the middle of the village. Built from limestone and ironstone in 1150, it is one of only three churches in England that have retained their original plan from the period. The characteristic Norman zigzag patterns decorate the walls inside and out, and the west front, one of the chief reasons for the church's reputation, has three superb arches. The interior is a model of Norman harmony, although during the Civil War, Cromwell, never a respecter of church architecture, used it to stable his cavalry's horses. The church was carefully restored by G.E.Street in 1862 (picture, p.126).

STOKE HAMMOND

Map p.150, A3
2 miles SE of Newton Longville on the A4146

The new estates of Bletchley and Milton Keynes have so far not spread as far as Stoke Hammond but they can be seen lapping closer from the hill that forms the high-point of this large village just off the Grand Union Canal. The church and the old part of the village are in a lane off the Linslade road and a number of thatched old cottages are scattered around the hillside. There is a 17th-century grey brick rectory near the church and and an 18th-century brick farmhouse at the junction of the village lane and the main road.

St Luke's Church, an early 14th-century building of limestone and ironstone, contains a font of the same era. There is also a communion table dated 1619 and a 17th-century pillar alms box. A monument to the Disney family with five kneeling figures stands against one wall and there is some 15th-century glass in the windows at the north end of the nave.

STOKENCHURCH

Map p.150, A3
2 miles SE of Newton Longville on the A4146

Stokenchurch has been relieved of most of the traffic that once passed through its centre, but the din of the M40, which skirts its southern edge before pouring over the Chiltern escarpment, is a reminder of its position on the main London-to-Oxford road. It is a large village, once a centre for chairmaking with an L-shaped green bisected by the A40. The houses are a mixture of styles in which the 20th century prevails. The Kings Arms Hotel, for example, has been given a rustic brick façade, clearly intended to 'improve' the 18th-century coaching inn it once was. The older cottages, built from the local flint, are generally tucked away out of view from the main road. The green is spacious, with a Methodist chapel of 1896, and a cluster of houses and three pubs in the middle.

The parish church is approached by a path from the north side of the green, and stands on the site of an earlier wooden structure from which the village derived its name – 'stoccen', meaning the stocks.

⛪ The medieval **Church of St Peter and St Paul** is mainly 13th-century, its flint walls partially hidden behind render and pebbledash. The tower, which is Norman, is hung with wooden shingles, with a green, copper clad bellcot on top, added in 1893 together with the north aisle. There are 15th-century brasses of two knights, both called Robert Morle, in the chancel. From the churchyard an uninterrupted view opens north-west over fields towards Crowell Wood, just over the Oxfordshire border, and an unsightly concrete communications tower.

STOKE POGES

Map p.142, C4
3 miles S of Gerrards Cross on the B416

The 18th-century poet Thomas Gray wrote many of his best verses while staying here with his mother, most famously his 'Elegy Written in a Country Churchyard'.

> *The curfew tolls the knell of parting day,*
> *The lowing herd winds slowly o'er the lea,*
> *The ploughman homeward plods his weary way,*
> *And leaves the world to darkness and to me.*

But those seeking herds, or ploughmen, or indeed anything of the idyllic, rural surroundings that inspired him will be sadly disappointed, for Stoke Poges is almost entirely suburbanized. The one exception is its southern extremity, where Gray's memorial, a sarcophagus on a hefty pedestal, stands amid a 10-acre field preserved by the National Trust as a reminder of the agricultural past. Nearby are a Tudor manor and a Domesday Book church, both of which prompted Gray to verse.

Directly adjoining the churchyard is a beautifully landscaped Garden of Remembrance. Its impeccably tended lawns, borders and avenues, which lead down to a serpentine lake, are well worth a visit at any time of year.

St Giles's Church has a good pedigree, with remnants of Saxon stonework incorporated in a basically Norman structure. There are many signs of antiquity, such as the 700-year-old door, brasses from the 15th and 16th centuries, and a 16th-century chapel which was originally built to serve the local almshouse. Separated from the church until the late 18th century, the chapel has a mellow brick floor, some 17th-century stained glass and an unlikely shrine to the 4th (Prince of Wales' Own) Gurkha Rifles.

Gray, of course, is omnipresent. There is his corner pew, the record of his burial and even a copy of his will. Outside, meanwhile, there is the yew beneath which he composed 'Elegy Written in a Country Churchyard'.

But there are also some interesting non-Gray touches. One is a pair of richly painted windows depicting a little girl's heavenward ascent from her earthly mother to a waiting angel's arms. Another is a fragment of stained glass in the west wall which shows a naked man blowing a horn

astride a bicycle-like contraption. Where does he come from? What does he represent? It is all a tantalizing mystery.

STONE

Map p.149, F2
2½ miles SW of Aylesbury on the A418

Much of Stone is strung out along the A418 from Aylesbury to Thame. But the more attractive part, which includes the church, is off the main road in the direction of the adjacent hamlet of **Bishopstone**. St John's Hospital at the western end of the village was from more than 130 years used as a mental hospital but the 'Care in the Community' programme has rendered it obsolete. Its Victorian red-brick buildings and chapel were designed by T.H.Wyatt and D.Brandon in 1850 and to the south command an expansive view of the Chilterns. The tiny hamlet of **Sedrup**, off the main road towards Aylesbury, is a collection of old and new houses with a farm on a green which has remain relatively unchanged for hundreds of years.

⛪ The 12th-century **St John the Baptist's Church** contains an intricately detailed font. Of the same antiquity as the church, it was actually brought here from Berkshire in 1843. Tub-shaped, it is decorated with bands showing birds, animals, human heads and fishes. One part shows men fighting dragons, the tail of one of which is knotted showing it has been subdued. The nave and north arcade of the church are also 12th-century and the south door has Norman zigzag carving. The west tower is 14th-century. There are several 15th- and 16th- century brasses .

STONY STRATFORD

Map p.153, D3
4 miles NW of Central Milton Keynes on the A5

Although now forming the most westerly suburb of MILTON KEYNES, Stony Stratford

remains a delightful place, altogether in a different class from its somewhat uninspiring neighbours. Its origins and its history as an important staging post on Watling Street – the main coaching route from London to Chester – are very evident, even in the late 20th century. The town is now by-passed by the new A5 trunk road, and the original Roman Watling St bears the name High St as it runs arrow-straight through the centre. High St boasts a number of old coaching inns, most notably The Bull and The Cock, about 100 yds apart, which are said to be the source of the original 'cock and bull' story. Other old inns on High St include The Old George, The Stratford Arms, The White Horse, The Fox and Hounds and The Different Drummer – all within a quarter of a mile. All have restaurants, and there are enough other good eating places in the town to make Stony Stratford the gastronomic capital of the Milton Keynes area.

Well-fed visitors may care to walk off some of their lunch by exploring some of the charming, mostly 18th-century, alleys leading off each side of High St. There are surprises down each one: interesting old buildings, pretty stone houses adorned with hanging flower-baskets, some fascinating, individual shops, the appetizing aromas of restaurant kitchens and, at the passageway alongside No 75 (on the western side of the street), a delightful, old-style coffee shop. All the inns along High St, and many of the shops, display hanging signs – and, in a reasonably successful effort to replicate the character of the High St and its old coaching days, so too do all the shops in the small, new shopping centre of Cofferidge Close at the street's southern end.

⛪ The **Church of St Mary and St Giles**, another of the ancient, cream-stone, square-towered churches so prominent in the north of Buckinghamshire, is on the west side of High St at its junction with Church St. There is a well-tended flower garden on the church's frontage to Church St.

♣ To the north of the town centre, at the end of High St, is the western fringe of the

Thornborough Bridge

extensive **Ouse Valley Country Park** (most of which is to the east of the A5, adjacent to Wolverton). The area next to the Great Ouse, from which gravel was extracted in the late 1970s for the construction of the A5 trunk road, has been imaginatively reinstated, and is now a Wildlife Conservation Area managed by the Berks, Bucks and Oxon Naturalists Trust, providing wetland habitats for waders and waterfowl.

SWANBOURNE

Map p.149, B3
2 miles E of Winslow on the B4032

Swanbourne sits amid a wealth of trees in the rural heart of Aylesbury Vale. Most of the original village was destroyed in the Civil War, and the majority of its black-and-white cottages date from the 18th century, although a few older buildings have survived.

⛪ The limestone **St Swithin's Church** on the main Winslow road has parts dating from the 13th, 14th and 15th centuries. Restoration work was carried out in 1863. The church also has a modern bellringers' gallery, a memorial to George V provided by parishioners in 1936.

A fine Elizabethan manor house stands to the west of the church. Near the manor house is **Swanbourne House**, now a prep school but once the home of the diarist Elizabeth Wynne. She married Thomas Fremantle, one of Nelson's captains at Trafalgar. His descendant, Commander John Fremantle, still lives in Swanbourne and is the Lord Lieutenant of Buckinghamshire.

TAPLOW

Map p.142, C1
4 miles W of Slough off the A4

Set on a hill above the Thames, Taplow has managed so far to fend off encroaching suburbia from nearby Slough. It preserves its village identity in a prosperous fashion, with red-brick, half-timbered cottages co-existing happily with Georgian houses and more recent buildings – although a slope of radically ugly box-dwellings does strike a jarring note. There are a number of big houses, the most impressive being **Taplow Court**, a brick and stone Victorian mansion on top of the hill, which was once owned by Lord and Lady Desborough. The roads north lead past a small vineyard to tracts of glorious beech.

⛪ The **Church of St Nicholas** is centrally placed by the village green. Its massive yews and eye-catching green spire presage great things, but the interior is slightly disappointing. Built in 1912 to replace an earlier structure, it houses a fine stone screen and some brasses dating back to 1459. To the north is the Desborough family pew whose walls carry a panoply of plaques to Scottish nobles. Names such as Orkney, Kirkwall, Breadalbane and Inchiquin come as an exotic surprise amid such Englishness.

More exotic still is **Taplow Vineyard**, next to the cricket ground to the north of the village, where a range of white wines have been produced since 1983. Both the vineyard and its winery are open to the public, and guided tours, complete with tastings, can be arranged. The best time to visit is between June and September, when the grapes are harvested.
Taplow Vineyard: All year, daily except Sat afternoon and Sun. Tel: 0628 29455.

THORNBOROUGH

Map p.153, F1
3 miles E of Buckingham off the A421

Thornborough village slopes gently northwards from the fast Buckingham to Milton Keynes road and an ancient bridge.
   The narrow 14th-century structure is the county's only surviving medieval bridge (picture, p.118). Its arches cross Claydon Brook and are just 12 ft wide, although the bridge is 165 ft long.

The village itself is a complex of tree-lined lanes, where willow and ash mask white-painted cottages, some thatched, set among a series of small greens.

⛪ St Mary's Church is believed to date back to Saxon times, and parts of it, including the chancel arch, are certainly 13th-century. It has a bright, spacious interior.

Older still are two huge burial mounds on the village side of the brook. Excavations in 1840 discovered immaculately preserved Roman coins, a bronze lamp with its wick still in place and a gold ornament decorated with an engraving of Cupid. These treasures are now in the Cambridge University Museum of Archaeology and Ethnology.

TURVILLE

Map p.140, A4   ★★
6 miles NW of Marlow off the B482

Turville sits at the bottom of one of the most beautiful valleys in the Chilterns, with slopes that rise steeply in the north to a narrow ridge, from which a smock mill overlooks the village. The valley bottom is dry, which probably explains its name: Turville is a spelling that was settled upon only in 1826, and its original may have been Therfield, which is derived from a word meaning 'dry field'.

The earliest evidence of settlement is Anglo-Saxon and in the 8th century, lands in Turville were given to St Albans Abbey. But its subsequent history has not always been peaceful. During the Middle Ages the well-wooded area was notorious as a shelter for runaway serfs and outlaws, and later, with the advent of the stage coach, it became a profitable hideout for the highwaymen who tried their luck on the Oxford–London route.

The present village, as appealing as its setting, is all situated within sight of its church, with cottages that are a a delightful mixture of rough flint, red brick and timber frames, most of them with gabled dormers jutting up into plain tiled roofs. In contrast, the Old School House is smartly built of knapped flints, with a combination of square, Gothic and round windows.

The Old Vicarage, adjoining the churchyard, has rustic flint decoration similar to that at BRADENHAM and is set next to a cottage whose adjoining barn has Gothic windows and a curious lantern light in the shape of an octagonal turret.

⛪ St Mary's Church★ occupies the site of a 12th-century structure but the present building dates from the early 13th century and has been much altered. The Norman door in its north wall has been blocked (see IBSTONE) and its 14th-century flint tower seems strangely dwarfed, even though it was raised in brick in the 17th century – at which time the chancel was also added.

The interior includes a steep, early 14th-century, king-post roof, and a north aisle, added in 1733 for use by the Lords of the Manor, which is separated from the rest of the congregation by an Edwardian screen. Within stands an imposing marble memorial to William Perry (d. 1740) and his family, occupants of Turville Park (see SOUTHEND).

Under the tower sits a large stone coffin with an intriguing history: When it was opened during restoration works in 1901, it was found to contain two skeletons. Among the gravestones in the churchyard there are some wooden, so-called 'bed heads' – inscribed planks on upright posts, also known as dead boards or leaping boards.

🥾 A footpath from the village leads to **Turville Hill**, passing a white-painted, weatherboarded windmill, similar to that at Lacey Green (see p.29) from where there are splendid views over the village. The path then descends the other side of the ridge through woodland, before turning towards IBSTONE.

TURWESTON

Map p.152, E1
7 miles NW of Buckingham off the A422

Turweston is in the north-west tip of the county, separated from the neighbouring

121

Northamptonshire town of Brackley by the Great Ouse and the A43 trunk road. It is a beautiful little place, somewhat gentrified, with limestone cottages nestling around the church; more modern, brick buildings lead into the surrounding farmland.

🛎 The **Church of the Assumption** at the north end of the village dates back to the early 12th century, with a Tudor roof. It has some fine glass windows, and interesting brasses and stone memorials, including a kneeling, 17th-century couple.

TYLERS GREEN

Map p.146, F4
3 miles E of High Wycombe on the B474

Poised at the edge of High Wycombe's urban sprawl, Tylers Green is appropriately dominated by a large triangular green, around which rows of flint and brick cottages lurk behind tall, clipped hedges. Its name hails from the medieval tile-making industry that thrived both here and in the neighbouring village of PENN – an association which is also recalled by the examples of Dutch gables to be found in both settlements.

The most attractive group of cottages is on a side lane, along the east side of the green, close to the duck pond. These include Cotters Barn House, set back in a large garden, and Old Bank House, brick built with twin dutch gables. On the southern point of the green is Old Laundry Cottage, with its low, flint-built laundry behind, now converted to a dwelling. The red-brick and flint school faces the green on the south side, as does Rayners, a large, red-brick house built in 1847 in the Tudor style.

🛎 **St Margaret's Church**, at the west end of the green, was built in 1854. It has a flint nave and chancel, with a separate wooden bell tower, on a flint base, that was added in 1891. The church was again extended in 1934, by lengthening the chancel.

TYRINGHAM

Map p.154, B2
2 miles NE of Newport Pagnell off the B526

Entrance to Tyringham is through an imposing, arched stone gatehouse situated to the north of the B526; yet it is easy to miss. Like nearby GAYHURST, there is no village as such at Tyringham, which comprises only the park land and former estate of Tyringham House.

Once inside the estate's arched gateway, the visitor is faced immediately with a straight, tree-lined avenue and a steep, menacing-looking, humped-back bridge over the River Great Ouse. Sheep graze the expansive water meadows, and the great house can be seen ahead, slightly to the left, a vista that is the quintessence of England.

🏛 **Tyringham House**, its bridge and gatehouse were built for William Praed in the 1790s by Sir John Soane. The gardens and the interior were redesigned and remodelled by Sir Edward Lutyens in the early part of this century. Soane's bridge remains a listed monument, and his entrance gate was described by the architectural authority Sir Nikolaus Pevsner 'a monument of European importance'. The house and much of its surrounding park land are now owned by a private clinic.

UPPER WINCHENDON

Map p.149, F1
5 miles W of Aylesbury off the A41

Once owned by Cardinal Wolsey, the parish of Upper Winchendon is spread along Main Road, which goes leads from WADDESDON to LONG CRENDON. It consists of a church, a few scattered farms, and **The Wilderness**, a long, two-storey house that is the kitchen wing (and all that remains) of a Jacobean manor house once owned by the Wharton family of WOOBURN. The first Marquis, author of the celebrated 17th-

The Music Temple, West Wycombe Park

century Protestant ballad *Lilliburlero*, is buried at the church but his son, the first Duke Wharton, took a different line. He gave his allegiance to the exiled James II, was duly convicted of high treason and forfeited the Upper Winchendon estates.

There is a small 18th-century Baptist Chapel at the North end of the village towards the Waddesdon crossroads.

🛉 **St Mary Magdalene's Church**, just off Main Road, is set on a promontory 500 ft above sea level, and has impressive views towards BRILL. The church contains a remarkable oak pulpit, probably 14th-century and carved from a single block of wood, a number of 14th-century decorated panels and 16th-century benches. There is a brass with a half life-size figure of Sir John Stodeley, vicar of the church, who died in 1502.

WADDESDON

Map p149, E1
5 miles NW of Aylesbury on the A41

Situated on the course of the Roman Akeman Street, Waddesdon featured in the Domesday Book as the manor of Miles Crispin. Through the ages it grew slowly, aided by its position on the junction of the roads to Bicester, AYLESBURY and QUAINTON. Then, in 1874, Baron Ferdinand de Rothschild arrived to build his towering new house of Waddesdon Manor (see p.22) at Lodge Hill just to the west. In the process, he briskly transformed the village.

He modernized its almshouses, established a literary institute and provided houses for the many estate workers that were needed to run his magnificent manor. Many of these buildings still bear the famous Rothschild monogram – five arrows and a coronet – on the front, as does the Five Arrows Hotel in the High St. Most of the land in Waddesdon is still owned by the Rothschilds, although a a couple of council housing estates were built here after World War II.

🛉 **St Michael's Church**, off the High St at the west end of the village, has a 15th-century tower, but some of its fabric is Norman. It contains an ornate alabaster pulpit bought at the Great Exhibition of 1851 by the Duke of Marlborough, first housed at the Duke's Blenheim Palace in Oxfordshire and then taken to his Waddesdon estate, which was later purchased by the Rothschild family. There is a large effigy of a 14th-century knight and a near life-sized brass monument to Roger Dynham (d. 1490), brought from the chapel at **Eythrope** a mile to the south when it was demolished in the 18th century. Two priests, Sir Richard Huntyndon (d. 1543) and Hugh Bristowe (d. 1588) are also commemorated in brasses.

WEEDON

Map p.149, D4
3 miles N of Aylesbury off the A413

The name Weedon probably stems from Woden, greatest of the Saxon gods; but despite its heathen associations, it was the first place in Buckinghamshire to be licensed for Methodist services and John Wesley himself was said to have preached at the village crossroads. Weedon's narrow streets surround a green where The Five Elms pub, a 17th-century thatched building, provides a village centre. The **East End** of the village is almost a hamlet in its own right and is made up of a number of attractive old buildings and a timber-framed farmhouse.

At the other end of the village there are some monastic ruins in the grounds of **The Lilies**, a country house which was the mid-19th-century home of local historian Lord Nugent. A fleur-de-lys can be seen in the house's porch, placed there in anticipation of the arrival of King Louis XVIII of France. However the Duke of Buckingham intervened on behalf of the Bourbon refugee and he settled in exile at HARTWELL the other side of Aylesbury. The village's oldest building is the manor farmhouse, which dates from the 1640s.

WENDOVER

Map p.146, B2   ★★
9 miles N of Aylesbury on the A413

Situated in a gap in the Chiltern Hills, this small market town suffers both from modern development and its position on the busy A413. Neither, however, has managed to detract from its essentially 17th- and 18th-century character.

Wendover is centred around its High St, a broad thoroughfare set on a long hill – where a market is still held – lined with ancient buildings, many of them timber-framed behind their Georgian façades. The theme continues in Pound St, at the top of the hill, where 18th-century grandeur mingles with the humbler outlines of small, half-timbered thatched cottages. The vista down the High St terminates at the Clock Tower, erected in 1842, which houses the Tourist Information Office.

Aylesbury St, leading north from the bottom of the hill, is a flanked by rows of unspoilt 17th- and 18th-century houses. There are no shop fronts, which partly explains why this part of town has survived intact, but its appearance is also enhanced by the variety of the individual buildings. On the corner is a long, early 18th-century brick building with a blocked central arch, the Corner House Hotel. Across the way is the 18th-century **Red House**, eight bays wide in plum-coloured brick, with a Doric doorcase. **Chiltern House** has a 1725 red brick front with gauged arches and a simple door canopy, but behind the façade is a 16th-century, timber-framed house with a carriageway leading to a yard at the rear.

The Grange is a late 17th-century brick house with gabled dormers. At the eastern edge of the old town is the 15th-century **Bank Farmhouse**, a blind-windowed red-brick house positioned on a steep bank above the road, beside a cluster of weatherboarded farm buildings. Over the road, in a street with the odd name of Coldharbour, is a picturesque row of white painted, half-timbered, brick cottages with steep, overhanging thatched roofs.

To the west of town, Pound St skirts the lower slopes of Bacombe Hill, where a narrow lane runs north to **Wellwick Manor**. The house has an early 17th-century front and an attractive group of weatherboarded barns of the same period. The ridge to the south of the manor connects Bacombe Hill to Coombe Hill (see ELLESBOROUGH). There are several good walks towards LITTLE HAMPDEN in the south and Chequers, two miles west of Wendover.

⌂ St Mary's Church is isolated from the town, on the edge of fields half a mile to the south. The best approach is along Heron Path which begins close to the Clock Tower, beside the Old School, a steeply-gabled Victorian building of flint and brick, which was converted to private houses in 1976. The path runs alongside a small stream overhung with trees, passing large houses set in spacious gardens. The church is originally 13th- and 14th-century, built of knapped flint with stone quoining. It has a square tower and side aisles with 14th-century arcades beneath a clerestory, but the exterior has a mainly Victorian appearance; it was restored in 1869.

WESTCOTT

Map p.148, E4
2 miles W of Waddesdon off the A41

Just south of the course of the Roman Akeman Street, Westcott overlooks Waddesdon Manor (see p.22) to the east. The large wartime bomber training airfield on the west side of the village is now the home of Royal Ordnance plc, which uses the base to test rocket and missile propellants, and many of the modern houses in the village were built by the Ministry of Defence to house workers at the factory.

Westcott was once served by the Brill-Wotton Tramway, a branch of which wound from Wotton to Waddesdon Manor. The tramway closed in the 1930s; the old ticket office and waiting rooms are alongside Station House, a private home, near the village school in the High St.

⌂ The **Church of St Mary the Virgin**, just off the High St, was provided by the

Duke of Buckingham (of nearby Wotton Underwood) and built by G.E.Street in 1867. It is a stone building with tiled roofs and a central bell turret. Inside, the roof is open-framed and the walls are made of patterned pale brick. The windows are plain glass except for one that commemorates the Duke's first wife Caroline, who died in 1874. Outside, some of the men of the former RAF Westcott who died in bombing missions are buried in the churchyard.

WESTON TURVILLE

Map p.146, A2
2 miles N of Wendover on the B4544

A spread-out village just south east of Aylesbury, Weston Turville was originally made up of four medieval 'endships': West End, Brook End, Bye Green and Church End.

Of these the most interesting is **Church End**, to the south of the village in the direction of Halton. On the north side of the church (in Church Walk) is a three-storey manor house which stands in the remains of a Norman motte and bailey. The old castle was dismantled on the orders of Henry II after the rebellion of 1174. Afterwards, it became the home of the Turville family, from whom the village gets the second half of its name.

The Georgian rectory alongside the church has yielded evidence of earlier occupations: excavations this century unearthed a Roman drinking vessel and a gold Viking ring, which are now kept in the British Museum.

St Mary's Church, in Church Walk at the south end of the village, has 12th- and 13th- century origins. Most of the glass was destroyed by Cromwell's soldiers when they occupied the area during the Civil War, but there are fragments of one 15th-century window depicting the Virgin and Child. There is a Jacobean pulpit and part of a 14th-century rood screen. The church

was restored in 1963 and there is a small museum in the north aisle containing relics discovered during the work.

WESTON UNDERWOOD

Map p.156, F2
1½ miles SW of Olney off the A509

'One of the prettiest villages in the kingdom' was how the poet and hymn-writer, William Cowper, described Weston Underwood in 1786, when he moved there from nearby OLNEY. Little has changed since then, as is witnessed by a sign at the centre of Weston Underwood detailing the 11 recent years – including 1992 and 1993 – in which it won the title of Buckinghamshire's Best Kept Village.

Listed in the Domesday Book as Westone, the manor house and estate of Weston Underwood became the property of the Throckmorton family in 1446, in whose possession they remained until 1898.

The house itself – Weston House – fell into serious disrepair and was demolished in 1827. All that now remains is a pair of imposing 17th-century pillars set athwart the Olney road, the stableblock with its cupola, long since converted to residential use, and the lodge. Formerly Weston Lodge, it is now better known now as Cowper's Lodge, for it was there that the poet lived from 1786 until 1795.

Just to the east of the village, is the entrance to the Flamingo Gardens and Zoological Park (see p.25); and to the south-east, across meadows and the River Great Ouse, is Emberton Country Park (see p.25), reached by road via Olney and the A509.

WEST WYCOMBE

Map p.146, F1   ★★
2 miles NW of High Wycombe on the A40

The old Oxford–London road, passing through the heart of the village, is all that

Stewkley Church

detracts from a harmonious collection of houses built between the 15th and the 20th centuries. The village street is sandwiched between a hill to the north, originally an Iron Age fort, and the 18th-century house and landscape gardens of West Wycombe Park (see p.23; picture, p.123).

The medieval manor of Wycombe belonged to the Bishops of Winchester and was acquired at the end of the 17th century by Francis Dashwood, a wealthy London merchant. His son, Sir Francis Dashwood, made lavish and much-admired improvements to the house and park, but brought a different form of celebrity to the village when he moved his infamous Hell-Fire Club from MEDMENHAM to the West Wycombe Caves (see p.29).

The village was bought by the Royal Society of Arts from the Dashwood family in 1929 and transferred to the National Trust in 1934. National Trust ownership, and the mere 200 yds of open road that still separate the village from the suburban sprawl of High Wycombe to the east, have been just enough to maintain West Wycombe's character and independence.

The **High St** is lined with an attractive mixture of timber-framed, brick, flint, rendered and tile-hung houses. The **Dower House**, built for Sir Francis Dashwood in 1763, is the old Vicarage. A Palladian-style house of decorative flint with an Ionic portico, set back from the street at the east end. The red brick St Paul's Church in the garden of the Vicarage was built in 1845. The George and Dragon hotel, on the south side, is an 18th-century coaching inn. The low, late 17th-century house beside the inn also has a carriageway and there is another timber-framed house opposite, **Apple Orchard**, with a jettied upper floor. The red-brick, colour-washed Manor House is early 18th-century, while nearby, again on the north side of the High St, is the late 15th-century **Church Loft** which bridges over the lower end of Church Lane. It is a timber-framed house with a jettied upper floor, used as a meeting hall, and a tiny clock turret.

Church Lane, which climbs the steep hill to the parish church, is also lined with irregular old brick and timber-framed houses. These include an old furniture workshop, with a red-brick lower floor and weatherboarded upper floors, which has survived from the 18th-century expansion of the chair-making industry in Wycombe.

St Laurence's Church★ is one of the most prominent landmarks in the county. It stands above the village on Church Hill, the southern spur of a wooded ridge, and is still surrounded by the single ditch that enclosed its Iron Age hill-fort. The church is medieval in origin and was once part of the hilltop village of Haveringdon, long since disappeared, but its 14th-century tower and long, 13th-century chancel are barely discernible beneath the lavish improvements made by Sir Francis Dashwood between 1751-62. The tower was heightened in 1751 and capped with a golden ball that is large enough to seat six people. There is a spectacular view from the top over the Wye valley. The nave was rebuilt in the grand, classical style, with giant Corinthian columns supporting a richly carved frieze and ornately painted ceiling. It was based on the Great Temple of the Sun at Palmyra, near Damascus. The low chancel ceiling includes the Last Supper, painted by Giovanni Borgnis in 1765.

The furnishings, which include carved rosewood stalls that resemble armchairs, and the font, with a serpent creeping towards the doves around its tiny bowl, appear to have been influenced by the Paganism characteristic of the Hell-Fire Club, an impression reinforced by the remarks of John Wilkes, one of the Dashwood circle, who pronounced the golden ball on the tower to be 'the best globe tavern I was ever in'.

The **Dashwood Mausoleum**★ (picture, p.131) is a large flint and stone hexagon, open to the sky, with niches for funerary urns set into its walls. It was built in 1764 to the design of John Bastard of Blandford. It is set below the church, in line with the new road to High Wycombe. The road was built using chalk mined from the caves directly beneath the church. From Church Hill there are wooded paths along the

ridge, north to the National Trust owned village of BRADENHAM.
Church Tower: *Apr–Sept, Sat–Sun & BH Mon 2–5pm.*
Church only: *Easter–Oct, variable hours.*
Tel: 0494 524411.

WHADDON

Map p.153, F3
7 miles E of Buckingham off the A421

Whaddon is a hill village in hunting country 500 ft above sea level, with excellent views overlooking the western edges of Milton Keynes. A mixture of older cottages, some thatched and white-painted, straggles round a dog-leg bend in the road, and there is some Victorian red-brick housing. Whaddon was for many years a self-contained village, but most of the traditional shops once found in its High St have closed because of competition from MILTON KEYNES, a common local problem.

The village is the original home of the Whaddon Chase foxhounds, started in the 19th century and now called The Bicester Hunt with Whaddon Chase. The hunt now meets regularly on farm land throughout Buckinghamshire and Oxfordshire. The word 'chase' denotes a section of hunting land detached from a royal forest, a status granted in this case by Henry III when the area supported 1,000 deer. Today only a small area of the original woodland remains.

The sandstone **St Mary's Church** dates from the 12th century with a clerestory added 400 years later. The interior has a number of impressive monuments, including the canopied tomb of Lord Grey de Wilton, one of the men who condemned Mary Queen of Scots to death.

The de Wiltons were early owners of the 16th-century manor house on the site of the present **Whaddon Hall**, to the east of the Stratford road which runs north as a continuation of the High St. Four different manor houses have stood on this site, one of them was home to the Buckinghamshire historian Browne Willis until his death in 1760 (see FENNY STRATFORD) In recent times the hall was used as a country club until closed by a fire. The building has now been converted into luxury apartments.

Due east from the hall is the site of the Benedictine Snelshall Priory, founded in the early 13th century. Only a few mounds in the grassy earth now testify to its existence.

WHITCHURCH

Map p.149, D3
4 miles north of Aylesbury on A413

A pretty village with many old houses, Whitchurch gets its name from the white limestone church on the hill. There are a number of black timber-framed houses, especially in the High St, where the pavement at some points is an elevated walkway above the road at some points. Market Hill, behind the High St, is the site of a long-disused market surrounded by stone and tile and thatched houses. Notable buildings include the timber-framed Priory (now a hotel), the 17th-century Whitchurch House with its diamond-shafted brick chimneys and the Old House on the High St and Oving Road junction, a 17th-century building with 18th-century stables.

The Firs, a mock-Tudor country house and grounds at the south end of the village is now the headquarters of a contract cleaning company. But during World War II, it was the home of the highly-secret government department MD1, or as it was more popularly known, 'Winston's Churchill's Toyshop'. Here, weapons for saboteurs and others were designed and built at the Prime Minister's bidding. Villagers became accustomed to hearing all sorts of explosions emanating from the test sites behind the house during and after the war. Little now exists to commemorate the role of the 'Toyshop', and because of its secret nature there are few references to it in histories.

129

The remains of **Bolebec Castle**, once a huge fortification are visible up the lane opposite the church. Walter Bolebec was an assessor for the Domesday Book and his efforts were rewarded by the Conqueror with the gift of the manor of Whitchurch. His castle, which stood in 16-acre grounds, was built here and held for him by a relative, Hugh de Bolebec. A spring on the east side of the site, which can still be seen, is known as Fair Alice after Alice de Bolebec.

The castle remained intact until the Civil War when the Royalists used it as a stronghold. Cromwell's army eventually took the place, however, and he ordered it completely demolished. The stone was used by local builders to repair neighbouring churches, houses and roads, and all that remains of Bolebec Castle now is a small mound topped with pieces of masonry.

Nearby is **Bolebec House**, the former home of the artist Rex Whistler. His picture, 'The Vale From Whitchurch', was painted in the back garden.

The **Church of St John the Evangelist**, of 13th-century origins, contains a large monument to the agriculturist John Westcar, who owned the nearby 300-acre Creslow Pastures which at one time was said to be the largest unenclosed pasture in the county. In former days Creslow beef had supplied the royal household of Queen Elizabeth I. Westcar, who died in 1833, was the first man to send cattle to Smithfield by the Grand Union Canal and his memorial depicts him in front of a prize bull, with sheep at his feet. Also in the church is a font dated 1661 with an unusual wooden plinth and a poor box, dated 1620, on the corner of a pew. There is 14th-century glass in some of the windows.

WHITELEAF

Map p.146, C1   ★
1 mile NE of Princes Risborough off the A4010

The hamlet is a pleasant mixture of small, 16th- and 17th-century, timber-framed cottages and larger houses, including an 18th-century pub, the Red Lion, which clings to the side of the Chiltern escarpment, backed by dense, old beech woods.

There is a steep climb from the hamlet to **Whiteleaf Cross**, a prominent chalk cross cut into the side of the hill. It is the largest of the chalk carvings in the Chilterns, but its origin is unknown. There are splendid views across the Vale of Aylesbury from the hill, with a fine choice of walks. These include one to the north east, along the Ridgeway path to Wendover, via COOMBE HILL, and others to Grim's Ditch and GREAT HAMPDEN in the south-east.

WILLEN

Map p.154, D2
2 miles NW of Central Milton Keynes off the A422

Approached via Dansteed Way or Tongwell St (respectively H4 and V11 on the MILTON KEYNES grid system), Willen is one of the old villages and towns now incorporated within the new city. Along with MILTON KEYNES VILLAGE, GREAT LINFORD and other ancient settlements, Willen is a good example of the positive way in which planners have tried to preserve the character of these rural communities. Newer properties within Willen village include up-market Regency-style, red-brick houses cleverly designed in keeping with their environment. From most of the village, however, can be heard the constant, low-level rumble of traffic on the nearby M1 motorway.

Immediately to the south are **Willen Lake** and **North Willen Park**, two of many green sanctuaries within the new city – some purpose-designed, some retaining natural characteristics from the pre-city days. Willen Lake is divided between North Lake and South Lake, the latter being largely a recreational facility for water-sports. The smaller North Willen

The Dashwood Mausoleum, West Wycombe

Lake, adjacent to the village, was built as a flood control measure to hold surface rainwater draining from the city's new roads. It now has a nature trail and is a conservation area already well-known to ornithologists. Its central island is a nesting sanctuary for ducks, geese, terns and redshanks.

On the western bank stands a **Japanese Peace Pagoda**, the first such structure to be erected in the western hemisphere. Completed in 1980, the pagoda was built by Buddhist monks as a symbol of peace and brotherhood.

🏠 Willen's **Church of St Mary Magdalene**, built in 1680 by Robert Hooke, an assistant to Sir Christopher Wren, is one of the most complete examples of a Classical-style church in the county. The large and impressive red-brick structure is in strong contrast to the cream-coloured stone medieval churches which abound in north Buckinghamshire.

The building was paid for by one Dr Busby, headmaster of Westminster School, and originally contained a small library to hold the books he donated to the parish. Vehicle access is to the rear, via Milton Road, but the front of the church is approached from Newton Road by a scenic, 200-yd footpath lined by mature trees, with open space to both left and right. By the church, standing in attractive and peaceful grounds spreading down to the banks of the north lake, is Willen Hospice.

WING

Map p.150, C3
7 miles NE of Aylesbury on the A418

Sitting on a low limestone hill overlooking Aylesbury Vale, Wing was one of the villages that in the early 1970s fought off the potential siting of London's third airport (see CUBLINGTON and STEWKLEY). Its seemingly appropriate name has nothing to do with flight, however: it comes from the Anglo-Saxon 'Weowungum', meaning 'Weowum's people', and the village was

settled in Anglo-Saxon times.

An 18-ft mound off the High St marks a Norman castle. In the 18th and 19th centuries the village was a stronghold of the straw-plaiting industry; in 1874 it came under Rothschild influence when Baron Leopold bought Ascott House (see p.14), and the family built it a village hall.

London's new airport was to have been sited at Wing airfield, still visible towards Stewkley and Cublington, to the north-east and east. A bomber training unit during World War II, it was one of the country's main reception centres for the repatriation of thousands of British and Commonwealth ex-prisoners of war during April and May, 1945. Now the runways and the few remaining RAF buildings have been taken over by factory workshops, private houses and farmland.

🏠 **All Saints' Church**, in Church St off the High St, was described by Sir John Betjeman as 'one of the most important Saxon churches in the country'. With its seven-sided apse and hexagonal crypt, it is certainly one of the most untouched 10th-century churches in Britain.

The church was probably built for Elgiva, widow of the Saxon King Edwy, who died in 959 AD. Most of the original building, in limestone rubble with stone dressings, has been preserved but the south aisle and west tower were rebuilt in the 14th and 15th centuries.

There are a number of monuments to the Dormer family, formerly of Ascott House, notably the tomb of Sir Robert Dormer (d. 1552) at the north end. There is also a 15th-century octagonal font and the remains of a 16th-century rood screen.

WINGRAVE

Map p.150, D2
5 miles NE of Aylesbury on the A418

Close to Ascott House (see p.14) and Mentmore Towers (see p.19), Wingrave has been much influenced by the residence of the Rothschild family at these two stately homes; the village school and around 30 of its houses were built by Hannah de

Rothschild of Mentmore in the 1870s for employees on her estate. In mock-Tudor style, they all bear the Rothschild monogram, the Five Arrows and Coronet. And the recreation ground, behind the central road junction of the village, was given by Lord Dalmeny (later Lord Rosebery) in 1924, one of the family who inherited Mentmore Towers from the Rothschilds. Next to it is a pond and the village green.

The Victorian manor house in the centre of the village was the home of Jan Masaryk, foreign minister of the Czech government in exile during World War II (see ASTON ABBOTS).

The Church of St Peter and St Paul, next to the village green, has 13th-century origins. Inside, there are 13th-century capitals on the tower arch and stone corbels decorated with wooden figures support the roof. above a 17th-century clerestory. On the north end of the sanctuary, there is a faded 13th-century wall painting depicting a shrouded soul being transported heavenward by angels. The tub-shaped font is Norman.

WINSLOW

Map p.149, B2
9 miles NW of Buckingham on the A413

Winslow is an old settlement: King Offa had a palace there in the 8th century, when its revenues were given to St Albans Abbey. Today, it is a small country town situated where the Aylesbury-to-Buckingham road crosses the Bletchley–Oxford railway, now largely disused. Although there is no trace of Offa's royal residence, Winslow still has some outstanding buildings.

The Buckingham road continues south to become Winslow's High St, with the parish church on the west side and the Market Place at the end, overlooked by some tall, handsome 18th-century buildings and flanked by the Bell and George pubs, where the local hunt sometimes meets for a stirrup-cup.

On the west of the High St, **St Lawrence's Church** is 14th-century, with a fine 15th-century porch. Inside, a clerestory illuminates a 15th-century oak roof and the remnants of a few medieval wallpaintings, as well as a statue of St Lawrence himself.

East of the Market Place is an excellent and surprisingly rare example of a humble baptist church, in this case built in 1695 for the Particular Baptists. Its first incumbent thought that children should be allowed to play even on Sundays, a heresy for which he was slapped into the stocks and fined.

West of the Market Place, the road turns very sharply left into Sheep St where **Winslow Hall** stands to the north of the highway. The seven-bayed, three-storey house, the finest in the town, was built in 1700 for the Secretary to the Treasury, Sir William Lowndes. It is a tall building, its height and solid elegance accentuated by four massive chimneys.

Past the hall Sheep St runs uphill and in just a little way is surrounded by open countryside leading to the hamlet of **Shipton**. Just on the bend and to the east stand two superb cottages with beautifully patterned brickwork.

At **Granborough**, two miles to the south, the 14th-century church of St John the Baptist had an unusual relic. In 1880 a rare 15th-century pewter chrismatory was found built into a church wall. The box held the holy oils used in church rituals before the Reformation. A replica is on display at the church and the original can be seen at Oxford's Christ Church Cathedral.

WOBURN SANDS

Map p.154, E4
5 miles SE of Milton Keynes on the A5130

The small, neat Victorian town of Woburn Sands sits right on the Bedfordshire border; indeed the boundary

line cuts through the southern end of the main street. Although rather large to be classed as a village, Woburn Sands was winner of the Buckinghamshire Best-Kept Village title in 1981 and 1984 – as is proudly proclaimed by a plaque on its Institute building.

The main street is distinctly one-sided, with shops restricted to the eastern side; across the road is the Institute building and a stone war memorial incorporating a small clock. From either side lead straight, narrow streets lined with rows of Victorian terraced houses.

The town is apparently a newer off-shoot of its neighbouring parish of Aspley Guise, across the county boundary, but the name of Woburn will always be indelibly associated with Woburn Abbey, the seat of the Duke of Bedfordshire, and the Woburn Wild Animal Kingdom, both of which are just a few miles to the south-east in Bedfordshire.

WOLVERTON

Map p.154, D1
2 miles NW of Central Milton Keynes off the A5

Wolverton is now one of three established towns to have been incorporated into the new city of Milton Keynes – the others being STONY STRATFORD, immediately to the west, and BLETCHLEY, some miles away to the south. Although the town has Saxon origins, in present form it is very much a product of the industrial revolution, especially since the coming of the London–Birmingham railway, which brought it considerable prosperity in the mid-19th century,when the London Midland Scottish railway company based all of its locomotive construction and repair there.

For a time, business boomed, and the town could boast the largest railway workshops in the world. But bit by bit, much of the work was transferred to other parts of the country – though Wolverton did retain its carriage works, which

eventually came under the control of British Rail Engineering Ltd. The railway works form part of an industrial area north of Stratford Road, adjacent to the main London-to-Glasgow West Coast line, which runs just to the east of the town.

♣ North of the industrial area, occupying the flood plain of the Great Ouse and extending westwards to Stony Stratford, is the **Ouse Valley Park,** one of several large expanses of open greenery and conservation planning within the city of Milton Keynes.

Here the **Iron Trunk Aqueduct,** opened in 1811 and one of the first of its type, still carries the Grand Union Canal over the river 35 ft below. With only two minor stoppages for routine maintenance in 1921 and 1986, it has carried the trade and leisure traffic of the canal across the Great Ouse Valley for getting on for two centuries.

To view the aqueduct from canal level, follow the towpath for about a third of a mile from where the Old Wolverton Road bridges the canal. There is a small car park there for the purpose, just on the other side of the bridge from the conveniently located Galleon pub.

Further down-river, about a mile to the east of the aqueduct and still within the Ouse Valley Park, the main line railway crosses the Great Ouse by a Victorian viaduct.

WOOBURN

Map p.142, B1
2 miles SW of Beaconsfield on the A4094

The village is situated in a steep valley on the little River Wye, where it sweeps down from High Wycombe towards the Thames. Half-timbered and brick houses are grouped comfortably around two sides of a large churchyard. They include the Harrow pub on the north side, Mulberry House, Boscobel and the small, knapped flint

Church Loft, West Wycombe

School House on the east. The Old School, a long flint and stone building with gables that are ecclesiastical in appearance, is now a row of private houses.

The southern end of the village runs into the outskirts of **Bourne End**, part of the general growth of semi-suburbia that has developed around a scattering of old farmhouses on the slopes above the Thames. Bourne End has some interesting river walks as well as a busy, largely modern High St.

⛪ **St Paul's Church**, Wooburn, although medieval in origin, is now mainly the product of Victorian alterations by William Butterfield. The long, knapped flint nave and tall west tower, with its octagonal stair turret, were restored in 1869. The simple, whitewashed interior, with its decorated, beamed ceilings, is from an earlier restoration of 1857. There is an ornate rood screen, designed by Ninian Cooper in 1899. The painting which hangs on the wall of the south aisle, is of Wooburn Green in 1888.

WOOBURN GREEN

Map p.142, B1
2 miles SW of Beaconsfield on the A4094

The large, tree-lined green is half a mile north of WOOBURN, on the southern tip of a ribbon of industry that follows the Wye valley down from HIGH WYCOMBE. The river once had a number of watermills working on it, and in the 19th century the quality of the water made it especially suited to paper making. The green is surrounded by a mixture of older cottages and Victorian or Edwardian houses, but is somewhat spoilt by more modern buildings, including shops and a mock-Tudor estate.

The Red Lion is a white-painted, brick pub on the west side of the green. It is joined to **Forge Cottage**, a jettied, timber-framed house with steep gables, on the corner of the road to nearby **Flackwell Heath**, where bungalows

hunch down comfortably behind high, protective hedges.

Wooburn Common, approached up a steep, narrow lane on the east side of the green, is a scattering of farms bordered by beech woods. At Odds Farm there is the Rare Breeds Centre (see p.26).

At the nearby **Glass Market** craftsmen can be seen demonstrating their skills working with decorative glass. The workshop is located in a 17th-century converted barn at Lillyfee Farm, off Broad Lane. The crafts on display include glass blowing and traditional stained glass, including glass painting and etching. There are weekend courses for beginners throughout the year, or visitors can simply watch the craftsmen at work. The workshop also carries out restoration work. It is sometimes necessary to carry out urgent repairs to the furnace and visitors wishing to watch glass blowing are advised to telephone before setting out. *Glass Market: Tue–Sun & BH Mons, 10.30am–4pm. Tel: 0494 671033.*

WORMINGHALL

Map p.144, B2
3 ½ miles W of Long Crendon on minor roads off the A418

The village seems, at first sight, to consist solely of residential estates, but behind these lies a scattered collection of older houses near the church. The Clifden Arms, a half-timbered, thatched pub, is on the other side of the village, beside Pond Farm, and is linked to the church by a path across the fields. There is an H-shaped group of almshouses, built in 1675 of brick with stone quoining and mullioned windows, in the Avenue leading to the church.

⛪ The **Church of St Peter and St Paul** is stone built, with a low, 15th-century, square tower, 14th-century chancel and 12th-century nave. The church at ICKFORD, just half a mile south-east of the village, can be reached by a footpath across open fields.

WOTTON UNDERWOOD

Map p.148, E4
8 miles W of Aylesbury on minor roads off the A41

Situated in the remains of the ancient forest of Bernewoode, the settlement of Wotton Underwood is made up of Wotton House and its grounds, a row of timber-framed estate cottages and a church. The remains of the Brill-Wotton tramway (see BRILL) are visible on the east side of the village.

Wotton House was the family home of the Grenville family, Dukes of Buckingham, until they inherited Stowe in the north of the county. The house was built for Richard Grenville in 1704 by John Keene on the site of a former manor house. A three-storey building flanked by two large pavilions, it was gutted by fire in 1820 and then again in 1929.

The grounds were laid out by Bridgeman and remodelled by Capability Brown, who later worked for the Grenvilles at Stowe (see p.21). They include a temple, bridges, grottoes and a double lake.

The house and grounds are private.

All Saints' Church, on the east side of the small green outside Wotton House, is a grey stone building with lead roofs.It has a 14th-century tower and in 1867, like so many other Buckinhamshire churches , it was comprehensively rebuilt by G.E.Street. Grenville family monuments are arranged in tiers inside the church and there is a marble slab in the floor with a brass set into it commemorating Edward Grenville (who died in 1585) and his wife. An Elizabethan effigy, in a recess in the west wall, is a belated monument to Agnes de Grenville who died in 1393.

137

Road Map Symbols

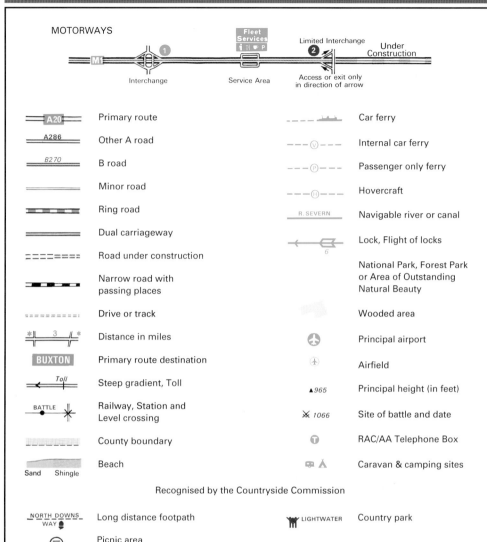

MOTORWAYS

Fleet Services

Limited Interchange

Under Construction

Interchange

Service Area

Access or exit only in direction of arrow

A20	Primary route
A286	Other A road
B270	B road
	Minor road
	Ring road
	Dual carriageway
	Road under construction
	Narrow road with passing places
	Drive or track
3	Distance in miles
BUXTON	Primary route destination
Toll	Steep gradient, Toll
BATTLE	Railway, Station and Level crossing
	County boundary
Sand Shingle	Beach

	Car ferry
V	Internal car ferry
P	Passenger only ferry
H	Hovercraft
R. SEVERN	Navigable river or canal
6	Lock, Flight of locks
	National Park, Forest Park or Area of Outstanding Natural Beauty
	Wooded area
✈	Principal airport
	Airfield
▲965	Principal height (in feet)
✗ 1066	Site of battle and date
☎	RAC/AA Telephone Box
⚏ Å	Caravan & camping sites

Recognised by the Countryside Commission

| NORTH DOWNS WAY | Long distance footpath |
| ⊕ | Picnic area |

| LIGHTWATER | Country park |

Scale 1:100,000 (approximately 1½ miles to 1 inch)

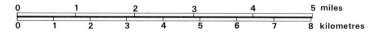

Cartography by Philip's
Copyright © 1993 Reed International Books Limited

The representation in these maps of any road, drive or track is not evidence of the existence of a right of way. Based upon the Ordnance Survey maps with the sanction of the Controller of Her Majesty's Stationery Office, © Crown Copyright.

Tourist Symbols

🅑	Tourist Information Centre	☐	Art collection	⛴	Historic ship
🅲	Tourist Information Centre Summer only	⬛	Art collection/museum	🐘	Zoo
⬛	House (N.T. if National Trust)		Ancient monument		Safari park
○	Garden	⠤	Earthwork	🐕	Farm park
◉	House & Garden		Windmill/Watermill	🐟	Aquarium/Dolphinarium
⬛	Castle		Other places of interest	🐦	Bird sanctuary/Aviary
▲	Cathedral	⊙	Roman antiquities	★	Viewpoint
✚	Abbey/Priory		Steam/miniature railway	►	Golf Course
✝	Church	⬤	Transport collection	BRANDS HATCH ▨	Motor racing circuit
⚡	Museum	◆	Military museum	NEWBURY ⚲	Race course
⚶	Local museum		Maritime museum	△	Youth hostel

Key Map

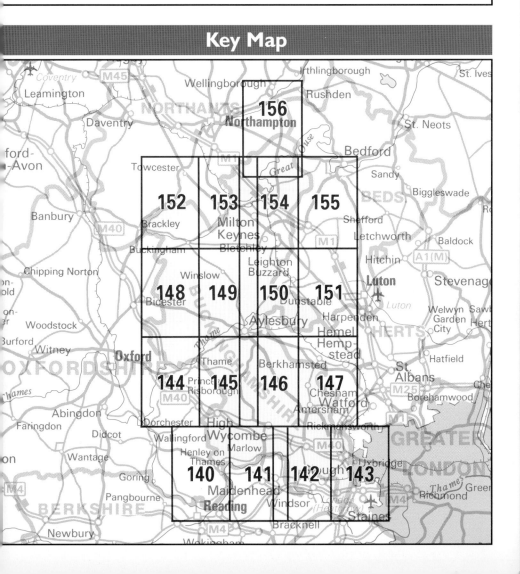

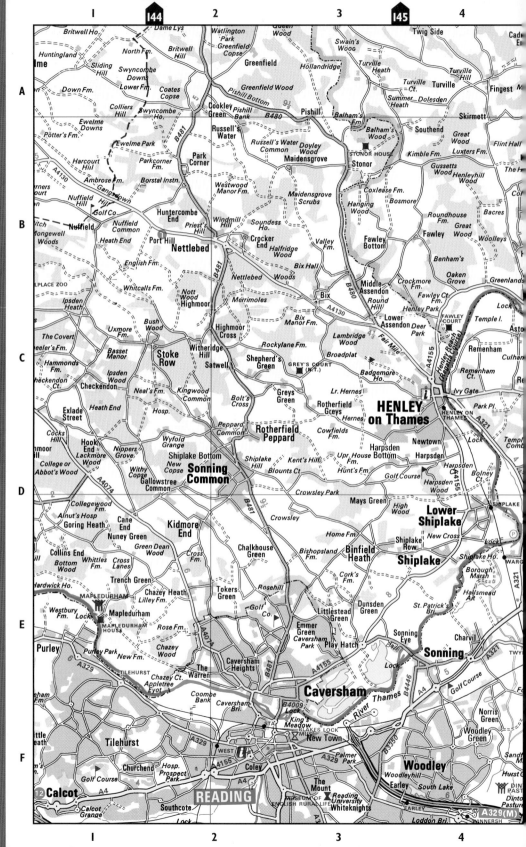

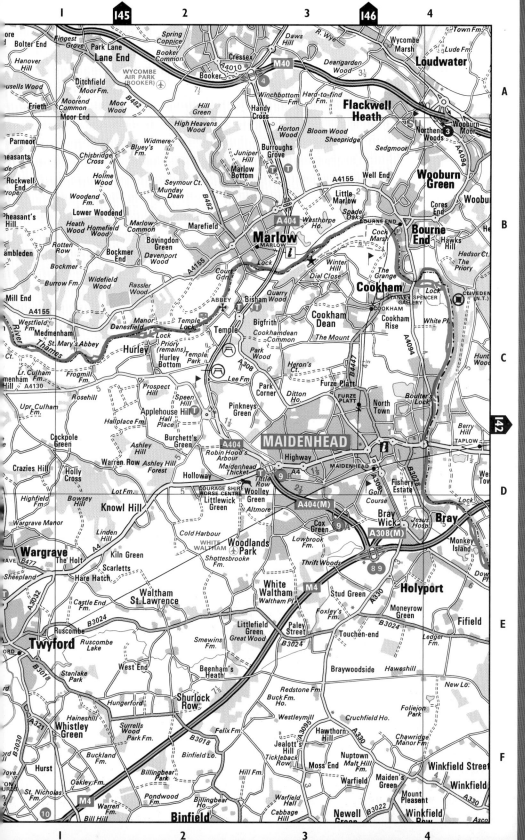

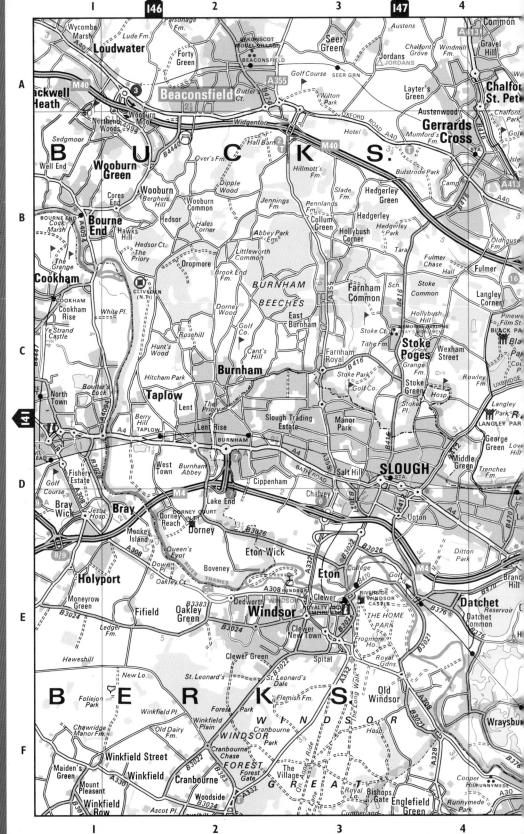

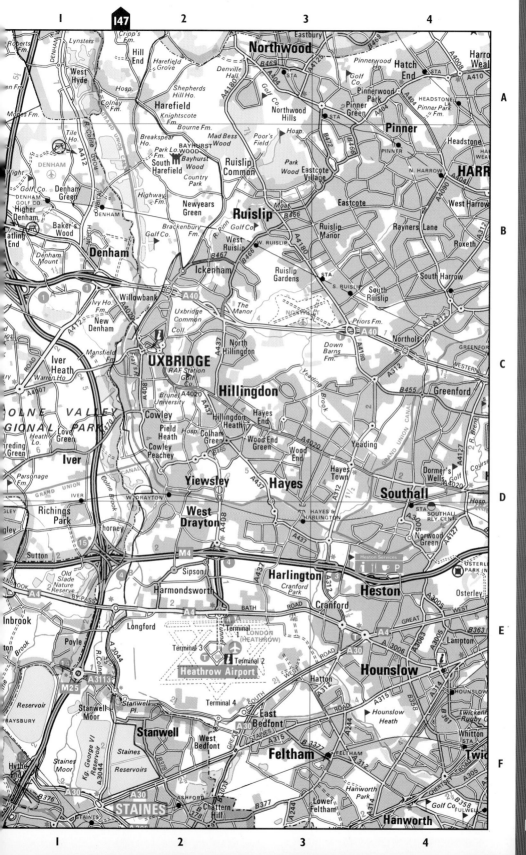

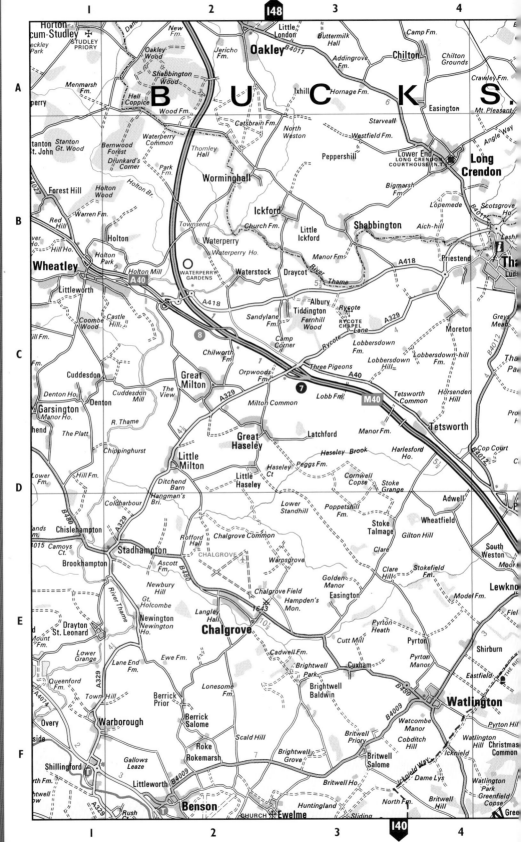

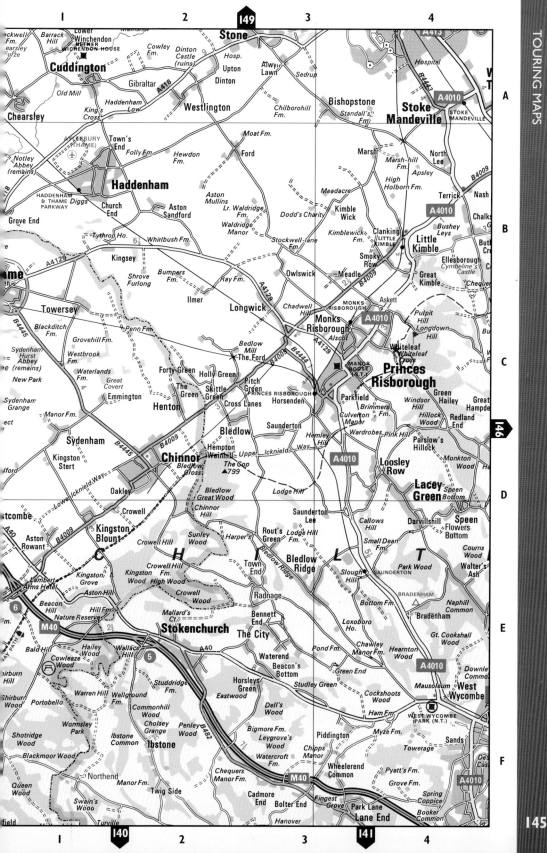

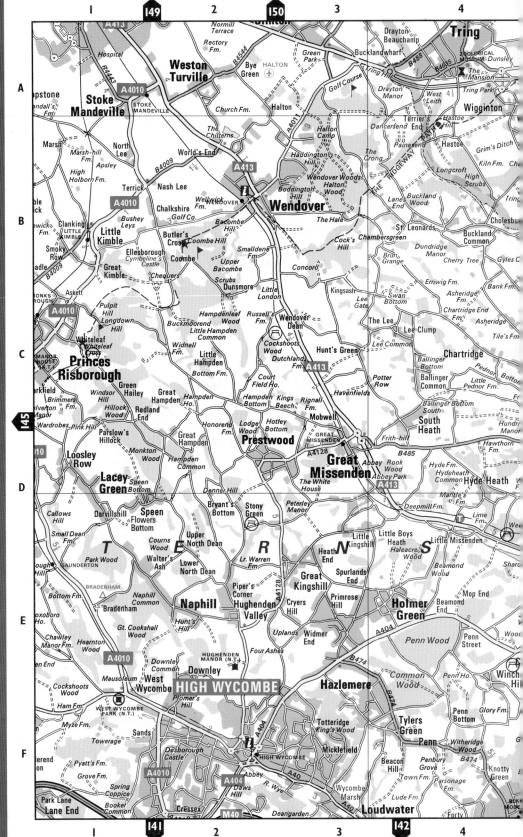

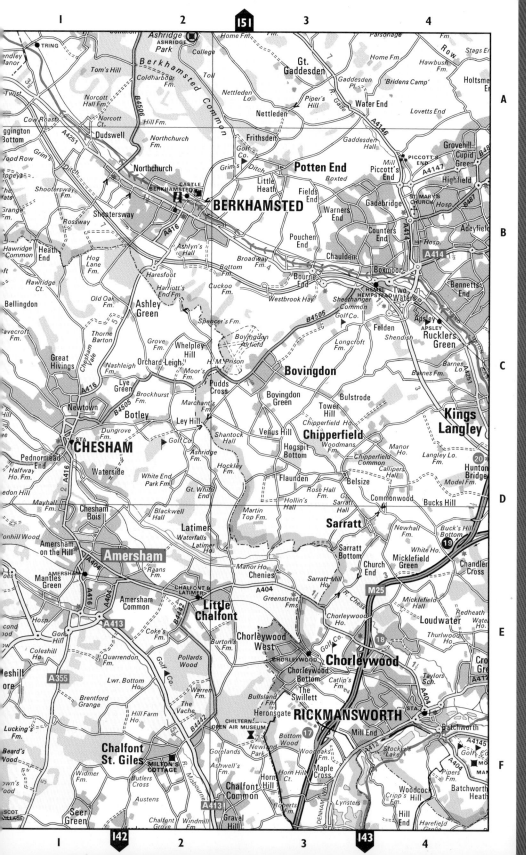

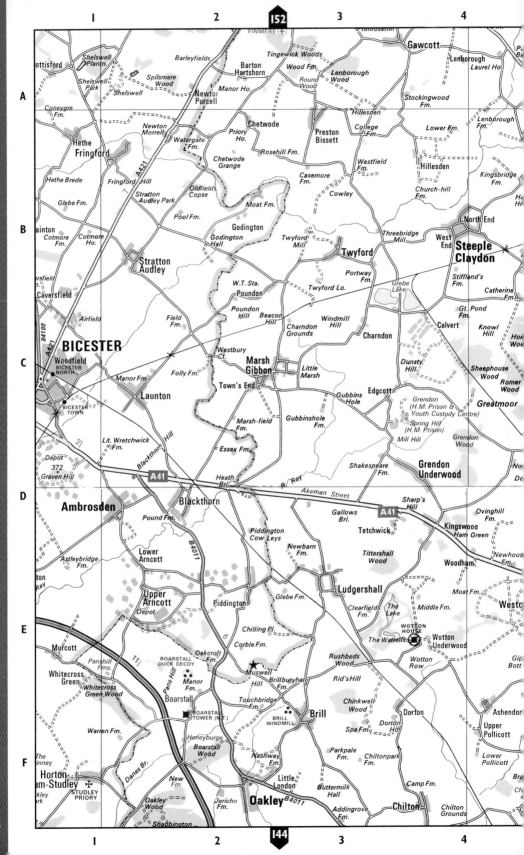

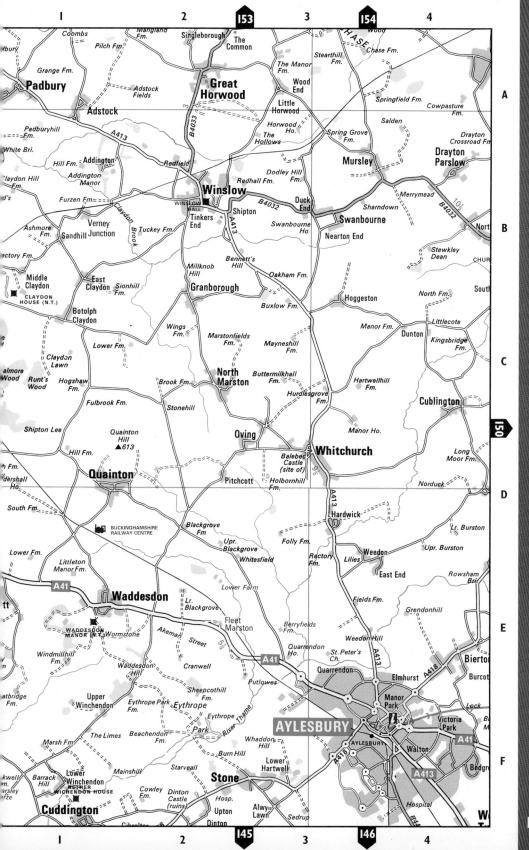

153 **154**

150

145 **146**

A

B

C

D

E

F

1 2 3 4

Coombs
Mangland Fm.
Singleborough
The Common
Wood
Chase Fm.

Pilch Fm.

Grange Fm.
The Manor Fm.
Stearthill Fm.

Padbury
Great Horwood
Wood End
Springfield Fm.
Cowpasture Fm.

Adstock
Adstock Fields
Little Horwood
Salden

Padburyhill Fm.
A413
Horwood Ho.
Spring Grove Fm.
Drayton Crossroad Fm.

White Bri.
Hill Fm.
Addington
Redfield
The Hollows
Drayton Parslow

Claydon Hill Fm.
Addington Manor
Redhall Fm.
Dodley Hill Fm.
Mursley

d's
Furzen Fm.
Winslow
WINSLOW HALL
B4032
Duck End
Merrymead
B4032
Nort

Ashmore Fm.
Verney Junction
Tinkers End
Shipton
Swanbourne Ho.
Swanbourne
Sharndown
10½

Sandhill
Tuckey Fm.
A413
Nearton End
Stewkley Dean
CHUR

ctory Fm.
Bennett's Hill
Millknob Hill
Oakham Fm.
North Fm.
South

Middle Claydon
East Claydon
Sionhill Fm.
Granborough
Buxlow Fm.
Hoggeston
Littlecote
Kingsbridge Fm.

CLAYDON HOUSE (N.T.)
Botolph Claydon
Wings Fm.
Marstonfields Fm.
Manor Fm.
Dunton

Claydon Lawn
Lower Fm.
Mayneshill Fm.
Cublington

Runt's Wood
Hogshaw Fm.
Brook Fm.
North Marston
Buttermilkhall Fm.
Hartwellhill Fm.

almore Wood
Fulbrook Fm.
Stonehill
Hurdlesgrove Fm.

Shipton Lee
Quainton Hill ▲613
Oving
Manor Ho.
Long Moor Fm.

Hill Fm.
Balebec Castle (site of)
Whitchurch

Quainton
Pitchcott
Holbornhill Fm.
9½
Norduck

dershall Ho.
Hardwick
Lr. Burston

South Fm.
Blackgrove Fm.
Folly Fm.
Weedon
Upr. Burston

BUCKINGHAMSHIRE RAILWAY CENTRE
Upr. Blackgrove
Rectory Fm.
Lilies
Rowsham Bri.

Lower Fm.
Littleton Manor Fm.
Whitesfield
East End
Grendonhill

A41
Lower Farm
Weedon Hill
Fields Fm.

Waddesdon
Lr. Blackgrove
Fleet Marston
Berryfields Fm.
Bierto

WADDESDON MANOR (N.T.)
Wormstone
Akeman Street
Quarrendon Ho.
St. Peter's Ch.
Elmhurst
Burcot

Windmillhill Fm.
Waddesdon Hill
Cranwell
5½
A41
Quarrendon
Manor Park
A413
Lock

Upper Winchendon
Sheepcothill Fm.
Putlowes
AYLESBURY
Victoria Park

Marsh Fm.
The Limes
Eythrope Park Fm.
Eythrope
Whaddon Hill
AYLESBURY
Walton
A41
Bedgr

Barrack Hill
Lower Winchendon
Beachendon Fm.
Park
River Thame
Lower Hartwell
A413
Hospital

WINCHENDON HOUSE
Mainshill
Burn Hill
Starveall
Stone
Alwyn Lawn
Sedrup
A413

Cuddington
Cowley Fm.
Dinton Castle (ruins)
Hosp.
Upton
Dinton

149

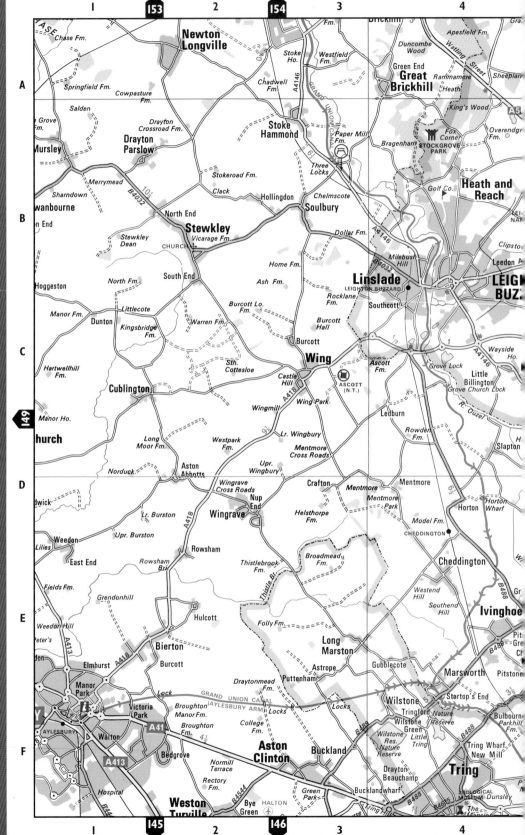

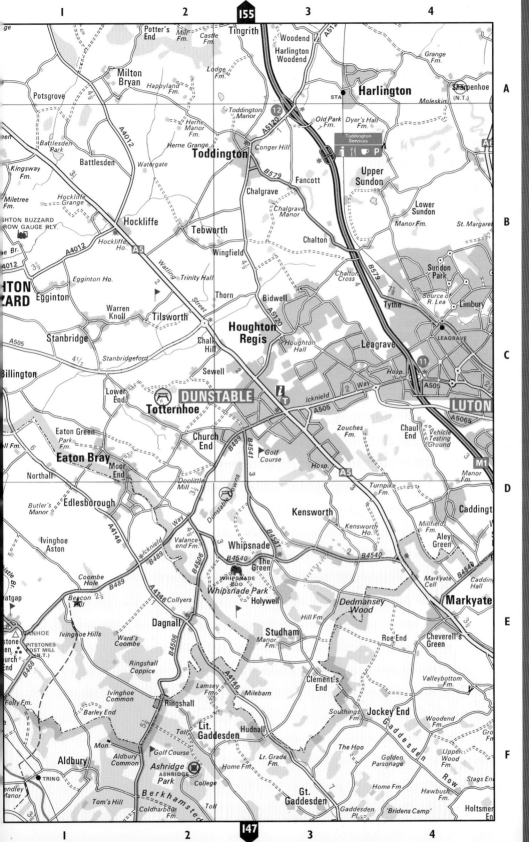

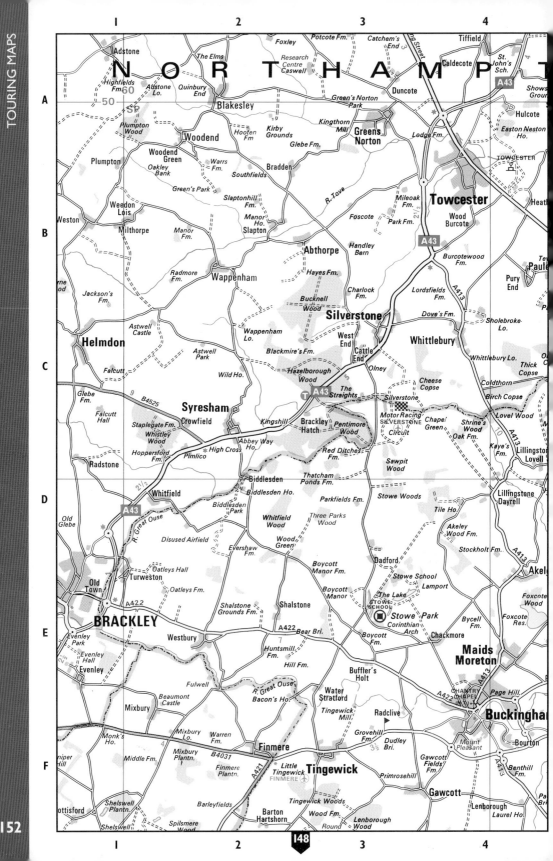

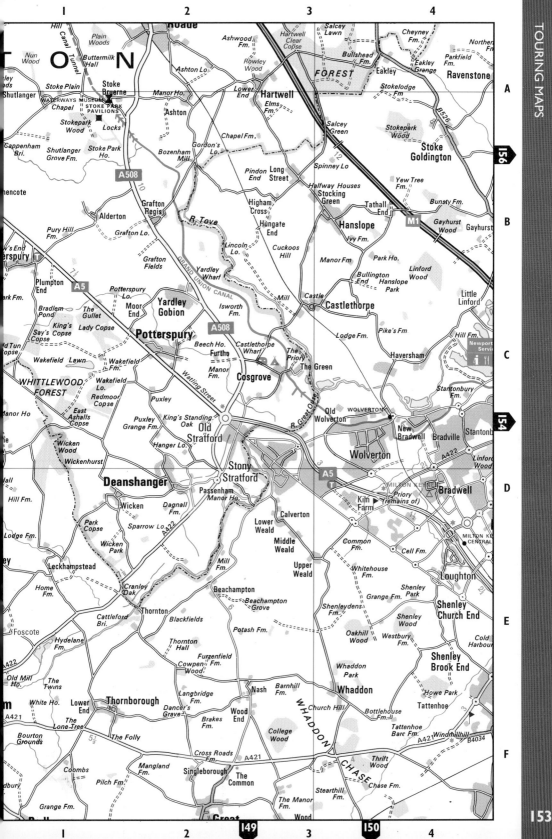

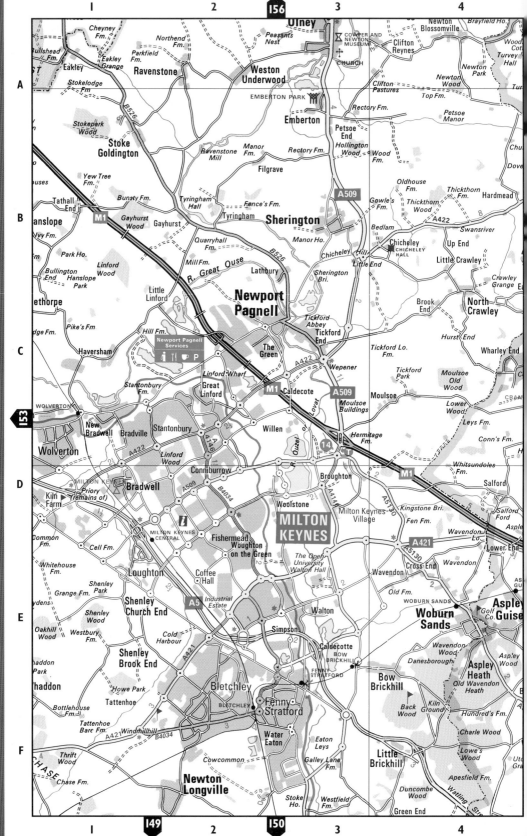

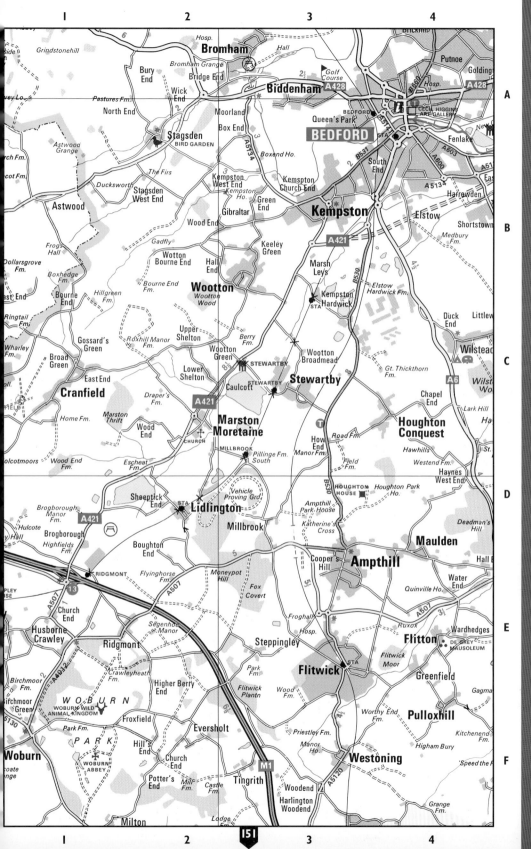

1 **2** **3** **4**

Grindstonehill
Bromham
Hosp.
Bromham Grange
Hall
Putnoe
Golding
A428
Bury End
Bridge End
Golf Course
A428
Bedford
Hosp.
A
Pastures Fm.
Wick End
Biddenham
Queen's Park
New
North End
Moorland
Box End
BEDFORD
Fenlake
Astwood Grange
Stagsden
BIRD GARDEN
Boxend Ho.
B531
South End
A5141
Harrowden
A51
The Firs
Kempston West End
Kempston Church End
A5134
East
Astwood
Ducksworth
Stagsden West End
Kempston Ho.
Green End
Kempston
Elstow
Shortstown
B
Frogs Hall
Gadfly
Gibraltar
A421
Marsh Leys
Medbury
Dollarsgrove Fm.
Wood End
Keeley Green
Elstow Hardwick Fm.
Duck End
Boxhedge Fm.
Wotton Bourne End
Hall End
Wootton
Kempston Hardwick
STA
Littlew
Bourne End
Hillgreen
Wootton Wood
Wilstead
Ringtail Fm.
Bourne End Fm.
Berry Fm.
Wootton Broadmead
Gt. Thickthorn Fm.
Wilst Wo
C
Wharley Fm.
Gossard's Green
Upper Shelton
Roxhill Manor Fm.
Wootton Green
STEWARTBY
A6
Broad Green
East End
Lower Shelton
STEWARTBY
Stewartby
Chapel End
Lark Hill
Ha
Cranfield
Draper's Fm.
Caulcott
A421
Houghton Conquest
Home Fm.
Marston Thrift
Wood End
Marston Moretaine
How End
Road Fm.
Hawhills
St.
olcotmoors
Wood End Fm.
Escheat Fm.
MILLBROOK
CHURCH
Pilinge Fm. South
Manor End
Field Fm.
Westend Fm.
Haynes West End
Sheeptick End
Vehicle Proving Grd.
HOUGHTON HOUSE
Houghton Park Ho.
D
Brogborough Manor Fm.
STA
Lidlington
Ampthill Park House
Deadman's Hill
A421
Millbrook
Katherine's Cross
Maulden
Hulcote
Brogborough Highfields
Boughton End
Cooper's Hill
Ampthill
Hall E
13
Flyinghorse Fm.
Moneypot Hill
Ampthill
Water End
A507
A507
Fox Covert
Quinville Ho.
A507
Church End
Segenhoe Manor
Froghall
Ruxox
Wardhedges
E
Husborne Crawley
Ridgmont
Steppingley
Hosp.
Flitton
DE GREY MAUSOLEUM
Birchmoor Fm.
Crawleyheath
Higher Berry End
Park Fm.
Flitwick Moor
Greenfield
irchmoor Green
WOBURN
Flitwick Plantn
Flitwick
STA
Gagma
5130
WOBURN WILD ANIMAL KINGDOM
Froxfield
Wood Fm.
Pulloxhill
Park Fm.
PARK
Eversholt
Worthy End Fm.
Kitchenend Fm.
Woburn
Hill's End
WOBURN ABBEY
Church End
Priestley Fm.
Higham Bury
Potter's End
Milf Fm.
Castle Fm.
Tingrith
Manor Ho.
Westoning
Speed the
F
Milton
M1
Woodend
Harlington Woodend
Grange Fm.
Lodge
A5120
A4012
A507
B530
A600
A603
A421

1 **2** **3** **4**

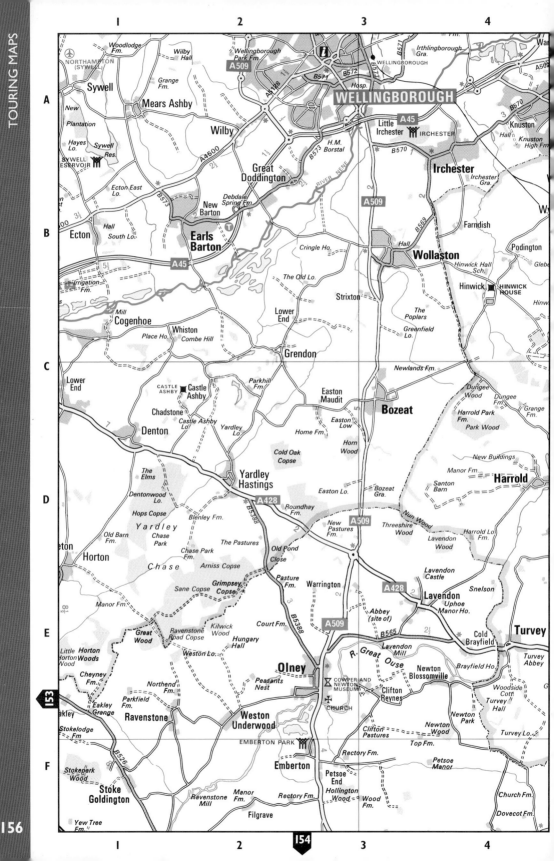

INDEX